Literary Theory and F.R. Leavis

# Language, Criticism and Culture: "Organic Community" in F.R. Leavis

Literary Theory and F.R. Leavis

# Language, Criticism and Culture: "Organic Community" in F.R. Leavis

M. SRIDHAR

*with a foreword by*

S. Viswanathan

PRESTIGE

*Published by*
Prestige Books
3/28, East Patel Nagar
New Delhi 110 008

1999

ISBN: 81-7551-058-7



*Photo Typesetting by*
Pivot Computers
Delhi 110 006
Ph. 3981867

*Printed at*
Chaman Offset Printers
New Delhi 110 002

# CONTENTS

# Foreword

Notwithstanding the imperfect sympathies of contemporary cultural-political criticism towards F.R. Leavis who wielded a deep and wide influence as a maker of the modernist critical era, quite a few books have come out on him in the recent years. Dr. Sridhar's book should not be docketed as yet another instance of book-making about Leavis, for it deserves attention for certain interesting and important perspectives in which it seeks to view Leavis's critical thought.

The book invites us to consider Leavis's abiding preoccupation with the intricate interrelationships between language, literature and the socio-cultural fabric. The idea of 'organic community,' an all but much-maligned concept nowadays, was perhaps, ultimately, something of a 'model' of thought for Leavis in terms of which to envision an ideal interrelatedness of culture, language and literature in society, an ideal nonetheless worth entertaining for its being a consummation devoutly to be wished for. Dr. Sridhar explores such postulates of Leavis about the 'subtle knots' that bind a 'cultural community' together. Sridhar's analysis leads him, among other things, to a discussion of Leavis's premise regarding the symbiosis and synergy between the individual and society, formulated thus in 'Literature and Society,' *The Common Pursuit*:

> You can't contemplate the nature of literature without acquiring some intuition in respect of that antithesis 'individual and society.'

Sridhar likens Leavis's assumption of a creative collaboration between the two to Mikhail Bakhtin's idea of an 'interanimation' of the individual and society. The later Leavis's use of concepts such 'the third realm,' 'nisus' and *ahnung*, no less than his early critical mission could be seen as a reinforcement of his pursuit of possibilities of a recreation, rather than preservation, of shared cultural values through the literary-critical endeavour. Such insights of Leavis regarding culture and community as well as language and literature, and literary study, are worth recalling amidst the prevailing prejudice against 'cultural community' in cultural criticism.

With English studies as the frame of reference, Sridhar distributes his attention fairly between Leavis's critical practice and theoretical assumptions, between the early and the later Leavis as well. The author sets his subject in worthwhile contexts; for example, he points to the probable, hitherto hardly recognised, influence of such an official document as the Newbolt Report of the twenties on Leavis's critical and educational thought despite Leavis's vociferous antagonism towards anything official. In sum, the book reminds us, in timely fashion, of the ways in which Leavis's passionate commitment to the role of English studies in the universities retains its relevance in and for 'our time.'

**Madras** **S. Viswanathan**

# Preface

There has of late been a lot of interest in what is known as culture studies. With the increasing importance accorded to the insights from history, sociology, anthropology and related fields in literary studies, the very character of language departments is undergoing a major transformation. Simultaneous with this development is the significant revision of our concept of language in the poststructuralist phase. Language now practically subsumes all fields of study. F.R. Leavis's critical output continues to engage our attention when we examine it in the light of these later developments. His firm commitment to the cause of English and his belief in its capacity to encompass culture, community and life as a whole need to be emphasized in this context. Along with it is his own particular version of history with its emphasis on the erosion of certain values consequent on the loss of the organic community brought about by the evil effects of technology. What he attempts, among other things, is a reconstruction of literary history from this point of view. Leavis's concept of the organic community thus seems, paradoxically, to bring together the two conflicting trends—of a community historically grounded in an imagined past as well as of a real community obtainable through a living language. Though Leavis introduces and discusses the concept of organic community very early in his career, it undergoes a continuous change from its being a mere historical phenomenon of the past externally invoked to study literary developments towards its being rooted firmly in the present with the language and literature, in a sense, encompassing life in its entirety.

Leavis's contribution to the development of English studies in England assumes special importance, especially when we consider the formative role of his response to literature in the shaping of his notion of language. His ideas of the role of the English teacher and critic, of minority culture and of the responsibility of the elite in society in training intelligence and sensibility among students take concrete shape in the context of the introduction of English as a compulsory university and school subject following the recommendations of the official report on the teaching of English in England (Newbolt Report). We can see a perceptible evolution in Leavis's conception of language through the decades. It is no longer just one of the many aspects of culture as he once believed. It now subsumes all traces of culture like individuals and their relationship with others, their beliefs, customs and traditions. Leavis sees in the nature of langauge a unique capacity to preserve shared values. Language and literature thus become for him an effective means to restore the values of the lost order of the organic community. Leavis assesses various writers in terms of their ability to represent in their work the lives of individuals and their relationship to the community at large. It will be interesting to see how this sense of collaboration Leavis would like to find in literary works compares with his own relationship with other practising critics. This book attempts to discuss some of these issues.

This book is a revised version of my Ph.D. thesis. I thank Professor Viswanathan for being an exceptional Supervisor and for helping me with the revision of my thesis. I have immensely benefitted from his scholarship and advice. I cannot adequately express my gratitude to him. I specially thank Professors Sudhakar Marathe and Mohan Ramanan for their involvement in my work and their helpful suggestions; Iswar for providing me with a copy of the Newbolt Report and other material not available in India; Sailaja and Nirmala for easing my tension over coffees and lunches; Murthy for helping me with typing the manuscript; all my friends, well-wishers and members of my family for prodding me; Chittappa for his meticulous reading of the final proofs and Uma for being the first respondent of all my drafts, for being at the receiving end whenever I was annoyed or frustrated and for finally seeing me through. And finally, I thank Prestige Books for readily accepting to publish my manuscript.

# Chapter 1

# Introduction

F. R. Leavis (1895-1978), son of a shopkeeper in Cambridge, rose from his middle class background to a probationary Lectureship in 1927 and battled through the institutional politics in Cambridge all through his teaching career till the termination of his Readership in 1962. A stretcher-bearer during the first World War, who chose to be a medical orderly because his "conscience" did not permit him to engage in direct fight, had to continue his indirect method against the Cambridge establishment, Marxist ideology, official channels of policy statement like the British Council, the Open University, and media such as the B.B.C. and *The Times Literary Supplement*. He found in *Scrutiny*, a journal he brought out for twenty years, an ideal medium to express his views and rally round influential opinion against his enemies. His own proposals for educational reform, his idea of the "English School" as the centre of the University teaching gained currency through the pages of *Scrutiny*. As a powerful classroom teacher Leavis had been able to bring under his influence many of his students who carried on his mission. According to M.C. Bradbrook, by the time *Scrutiny* was closed, Leavis's methods "had gone into schools, and into the remoter parts of the Commonwealth—India, South Africa, Sydney and even West Africa became centres of what began to be termed Leavisite teaching. In the United States he had long enjoyed a high esteem, strengthened by the New Criticism that arrived in the late forties."[1] Leavis did not fight a battle, though as a clever strategist he did draw "lines" of development in a major reorganization of literary forces from the seventeenth century onwards. He had been heavily influenced by Eliot and Richards through their ideas of the "common pursuit" of true judgement and "practical criticism" (in that order), yet had serious differences with both (in the same order). Though a student of history, he opposed F.W. Bateson's attempt to impose history over literature. Yet, he recommended a study of the seventeenth century as a key passage in the history of civilization and liked to assess the value of literature and culture in terms of the organic community-relations prior to this phase of modern culture. He developed his own ideas of culture, community, language and literature through the whole body of his criticism. His emphasis on the actual experience of life as well as literature prevented him from making any theoretical formulations of his ideas. In his quarrel with René Wellek, after Wellek attempted to explicitly state the principles underlying his criticism, Leavis refused to accept such reduction of his critical practice. As a literary critic, he declared himself as an anti-philosopher. However, he did recognize the need by the 70s to justify his theoretical position by drawing heavily on philosophers of science such as Michael Polanyi and Marjorie Grene. Though he had been opposed to the effects of science in terms of the technologico-Benthamite civilization, his direct confrontation with science occurred in his response to C.P. Snow in the Two Cultures debate and in his attack of Snow's preference for scientific culture. This perhaps instigated Leavis to come down heavily on the basic philosophical assumptions underlying scientific thinking. He went on to attack the whole of Western philosophy founded on Descartian principles in his later books like *Nor Shall My Sword* and *The Living Principle.* He took this opportunity to attack the scientific basis of linguistic studies too. His "incompatible" relations with Wittgenstein come to mind here. He came out with his own philosophy of language in its relation to culture, community and life. Together, his quarrels with many of his contemporaries helped him to defend, reflect and reformulate his own theoretical position and even strengthen it. As an English critic. his attempt has been to establish English at the centre of all intellectual activity. His intellectual battles with people in other disciplines reflect this enthusiasm. Even as he undermines the importance of various fields of study, he is anxious to emphasize the unique capacity of English language and literature to bring them all under its umbrella. As a critic, Leavis has consistently criticized coterie culture and manipulation of literary taste by the Bloomsbury group. Yet, he himself promotes and insists on the inevitability of minority culture to arrest corruption of standards. His idea of the English School and the training of the elite through critical activity contributes precisely to the domination of a small group. These various controversies surrounding Leavis's life and certain inherent contradictions in him help us understand the complexities of his critical vision. The present book attempts to examine the complexities through a study of the concept of the organic community.

In spite of a large corpus of criticism including some book-length studies on his work, not much attention has been paid to the idea of organic community and its role in Leavis's cultural thought and criticism. There has been a tendency even among the few who have studied this aspect to dub the organic community as a nostalgic, pastoral dream and condemn it as a myth. An attempt has been made in the following chapters to deal with the centrality of this concept which not only informs Leavis's views on language, literature, community and culture, but functions as a tacit criterion throughout his practical criticism. The idea of the loss of an organic community culture and values as a consequence of industrialization and the felt urgency to meet this particular challenge inform Leavis's thought and criticism. Leavis is also very much a part of that socio-cultural-critical tradition of writers like Coleridge, Arnold, Carlyle and Eliot (to mention just a few) who have addressed this problem. There has been some criticism on the impact of Arnold and Eliot on Leavis, influences Leavis himself has openly acknowledged. Factors such as Leavis's own immediate compulsions, his personal involvement in World War I, the anti-German stance which arose as a result of the War, the nationalist fervour culminating in the importance given to the study of English, combined with the growing resistance of the middle and lower classes to the study of the Classics traditionally reserved for the rich, have also been given some attention. However, the very obvious connection in this context between Leavis and the official report on the teaching of English in England (known as the Newbolt Report, 1921) has curiously been almost ignored. A discussion in this regard is therefore felt necessary, particularly in view of the fact that even Leavis chooses not to openly discuss the report, but mentions it only in passing. Leavis finds the atmosphere in which emphasis was being given to the study of English quite congenial to promote his idea of the organic community and the values associated with it. Through a study of a great tradition of writers, he hopes to inculcate these values. His own contribution to the tradition of the idea of the organic community, with his emphasis on the study of English and the training of men's sensibility and intelligence, discrimination, perception and judgement, has been underlined in the second chapter.

Another theme worth studying in Leavis is his recurrent and consistent refusal to theorize on the principles underlying his criticism. The Leavis-Wellek controversy on this matter, with Wellek's attempt to list Leavis's critical criteria and Leavis's denial of such easy reduction is all too familiar. Critics like Perry Anderson have attempted to see Leavis's anti-theoretical stance as a reflection of his adherence to a certain empiricism.[2] Terry Eagleton tries to relate Leavis's practice to a narrow mimeticism which looks upon words as things.[3] There has also been a tendency among some critics to reduce Leavis to a mere New Critic who gives importance to the words on the page. Few critics have tried to understand the interrelation of the various recurrent critical terms Leavis employs such as tradition, culture, community, concreteness, selfhood, identity, nisus and *ahnung*, or to view them in relation to his concern for preserving certain values. The individual-social coalescence in Leavis wherein he sees an individual's experience as being necessarily social and the values as inevitably shared ones has largely been sidelined. The third chapter therefore undertakes an indepth study of the various undercurrents beneath his critical terminology. It explains how the idea of collaboratively-creative critical practice becomes an alternative to the loss of organic community. The interconnections of Leavis's ideas on language, literature, culture, community and life, and the theoretical underpinnings of the concept of the organic community behind these ideas are discussed at length. An attempt has been made to tease out a loosely formulated theory, notwithstanding Leavis's assertion of being anti-philosophical. The chapter discusses Leavis's explicit use, especially in his later work, of philosophers like Michael Polanyi and Marjorie Grene, to give a concrete shape to his thinking. It also suggests how Leavis's theory of language compares with other contemporary theories of language.

Leavis also insists that a great novelist knows that a serious and developed study of the individual cannot but be a study of lives in relation and of the social conditions. This inter-animating emphasis of the individual and the social is rooted in his concept of the organic community, where the lives of men in relation to one another as well as to their culture and environment are strongly emphasized. Leavis's theory is tested against his practical criticism of the poets and novelists in the fourth chapter. The chapter shows how the life-principle operates as an all-pervasive criterion in his critical practice. How Leavis employs "life" and other related terms with subtle distinctions in his criticism of poetry and the novel and how these distinct ways could be connected to the historical development of Leavis's concept of language come up for discussion. The chapter also raises the question of the theory-practice mismatch.

The last chapter studies some critical responses to Leavis on issues connected with the aspect of the organic community (in the context of paucity of criticism specifically on this aspect) with the intent of arriving at some tentative judgements on Leavis's work. Questions such as Leavis's programme of education, his practical criticism, his training of the elite, the collaborative critical endeavour in theory and practice, the historicity of the organic community as well as its literary manifestation in the "living speech" of the writers are reexamined in the light of various critical responses. This chapter also takes into consideration the analysis of the complexity and the multi-dimensionality of Leavis's critical thought and practice (undertaken during the course of the chapters) to indicate how he defies any existing theoretical categorizations.

## NOTES

1. M.C. Bradbrook, "'Nor Shall My Sword': The Leavises' Mythology," *The Leavises: Recollections and Impressions*, ed. Denys Thompson (Cambridge: Cambridge University Press, 1984) 27.
2. Perry Anderson, "Components of the National Culture," *English Questions* (London: Verso, 1992) particularly 96-103.
3. Terry Eagleton, *Literary Theory* (Oxford: Basil Blackwell, 1983) 57.

# Chapter 2

# Leavis and the Beginnings of English Studies

> What was at stake in English Studies was less English *literature* than *English* literature: our great 'national poets' Shakespeare and Milton, the sense of an 'organic' national tradition and identity to which new recruits could be admitted by the study of humane letters.
>
> (Terry Eagleton, *Literary Theory*, 1983, 28)

Leavis's ideas on liberal education and on the centrality of English studies as a University (and School) discipline supplying a national need in the context of industrialization and its effect on culture, and his convictions regarding the role of the intelligentsia in fighting forces of disintegration can be seen to have an eminently traceable relationship to the Newbolt Report (1921) and to the various developments of about half a century preceding it. The Newbolt-Leavis connection has surprisingly received little attention from critics on English studies. Among critics writing on Leavis, Geoffrey Strickland does see a connection between Arnold, the Newbolt Report and Leavis and hints at their differences in terms of their emphasis on the study of English.[1] However, he does not accord much attention to certain similarities between the Newbolt Report and Leavis in their commitment to the cause of English. It is also interesting to note that Leavis himself makes only passing remarks on an important document like this.[2] This is understandable, considering Leavis's prejudice against anything governmental, official or institutional, all of which the Report was. This also goes with Leavis's distaste for the Establishment in Cambridge, the B.B.C., the British Council, etc. However, this chapter attempts to look at, among other influences, the Report in terms of Leavis's ideas on education and culture, and see how together they eventually lead to his views on criticism.

The beginnings of the interest in the formal study of English can be traced to the middle of the nineteenth century starting with the middle class resistance to the study of the Classics. The middle class opposition to the dominance of the aristocracy takes on two forms: (i) emphasizing the need to study science and (ii) the study of English as a humanizing force.[3] Matthew Arnold in his *Culture and Anarchy* advocates the introduction of English literature at every level in the schools, while retaining a reformed teaching of the Classics in the public schools.[4] Brian Doyle, in his "Invention of English" identifies the period between 1880 and 1920 when various strategies were employed "to combine the traditions of aristocratic cultural mystique with utilitarian programmes" for "educating, governing, and mobilizing a majority population to serve Imperial mission at home and abroad."[5] A coherent pattern of an overall, organized attempt at a promotion of a nationalistic fervour may be seen to govern such developments as the Settlement movement of the 1880s and the 1890s, the growth of a "provincial" college sector outside the ancient universities of Oxford and Cambridge after 1880, the foundation of the English Association in 1907, the delivery of education at the door steps through the National Home Reading Union, preservation of the rural landscape (under the National Trust in 1895) and art (with the starting of the National Gallery of Modern Art in 1897), the establishment of the National Portrait Gallery (1896), and the publication of *Dictionary of National Biography* (1895-1900), *Cambridge History of English Literature* (1907-1916), and *New English Dictionary* (1884-1928). Such a view has been taken by Brian Doyle among others. In the sphere of English education, whatever was taught in the departments of either English Language and Literature or English and History prior to the 1880s had mainly been "Rhetoric" with emphasis on historical and philological studies. English in its new form, on the other hand, was to emphasize the study of the works of great writers and in the drawing up of a list of such works as prescribed by a circular of the Board of Education in 1910.[6] The English Association established firm contacts with the Board and convinced it of the need for constituting a Departmental Committee to investigate into the status of English and to propose plans for future development. Eight of the fourteen members of the Committee when it was set up were to be the members of the Association. Commenting on the constitution and the interests of the association, Doyle says that it was

> . . . not so much as a pressure-group founded to further the professional interests of teachers of English, but rather a class-based mobilization which drew in not only most professors of English language and literature, but also like-minded politicians, administrators and 'men-of-letters.'[7]

The members, according to Doyle, devised strategies to check the potential dangers arising from "the loss of aristocratic leadership, and the rise of a cultural market place."[8] While the object in the case of the elementary level pupils was that of instilling "a feeling for the grandeur of the national language and literature," for the higher classes it was "to provide indirect moral inculcation through pleasurable and even joyous responses to literary values."[9] English was felt to bring the disparate interests within the nation into a single organic unity because of its "apparent potential to reach directly to the roots of subjective human response through modes of 'appreciation.'"[10] Efforts of this kind on the part of the Board as well as the English Association culminated in the writing of a Report by the Departmental Committee, known as the Newbolt Report.

The Report, also known as *The Teaching of English in England*, was published in 1921. Despite the victory, the war seems to have provided England with an opportunity to look back on its educational system. Voicing the superiority of the Germans on this front, Lloyd George says:

> The most formidable institution we had to fight in Germany was not the arsenals of Krupps or the yards in which they turned out submarines, but the schools in Germany. They were our most formidable competitors in business and our terrible opponents in war. An educated man is a better worker, a more formidable warrior, and a better citizen. That was only half comprehended before the war.[11]

A year before Lloyd George voiced this view, at Cambridge members of the Senate met to debate on the formation of an English Tripos even as "'Russia was tottering into revolution and America preparing for war. . . .'"[12] By May 1919, when the Departmental Committee was appointed by the President of the Board of Education, to inquire into the position of English in the educational system of England,[13] the necessity to promote a sense of national cultural coherence was already deeply felt. The terms of reference of the Committee, therefore, underline the duty to advise how its study may best be promoted in schools of all types including Continuation schools, and in Universities and other Institutions of Higher Education.[14]

The authors of the Newbolt Report define education as guidance in the acquiring of experience. They underline the importance of human relations in gaining this experience. In this context, English literature is seen as a study of a record of human experience. They also emphasize the importance of the study of English language vis-a-vis other subjects:

> If progress is not made at one time in the region of arithmetic or history or geography, the child merely remains backward in that respect, and the deficiency can be made up later. But a lack of language is a lack of the means of communication and of thought itself. Moreover, among the vast mass of the population, it is certain that if a child is not learning good English he is learning bad English, and probably bad habits of thought; and some of the mischief done may never afterwards be undone.[15]

Similarly, the primacy of English for a national education is most clearly spelt out:

> . . . we state what appears to us to be an incontrovertible primary fact, that for English children no form of knowledge can take precedence of a knowledge of English, no form of literature can take precedence of English literature; and that the two are so inextricably connected as to form the only basis possible for a national education.[16]

The authors of the Report deplore the fact that the "[i]dea of liberal education is either altogether ignored or struggles feebly for the right of existence . . . "[17] because of the predominant emphasis in public schools on the study of Latin and Greek. But not everybody has access to the public school and hardly any body has access to Latin and Greek. It is here that the authors recognise the importance of English in its ability to provide "a channel of supply" of "experience to be found in great art" which is "within the reach of all without distinction."[18] Developing the metaphor of the "channel" they go on:

> Moreover, if we explore the course of English literature, if we consider from what sources its stream has sprung, by what tributaries it has been fed, and with how rich and full a current it has come down to us, we shall see that it has other advantages not to be found elsewhere. There are mingled in it, as only in the greatest of rivers there could be mingled, the fertilizing influences flowing down from many countries and from many ages of history. Yet all these have been subdued to form a stream native to our own soil. *The flood of diverse human experience which it brings down to our own life and time is in no sense or degree foreign to us, but has become the native experience of men of our own race and culture.*[19] (Emphasis added)

They are convinced that for "a full measure of culture and humane training," English must form "the essential basis of a liberal education for all English people."[20]

Doyle sees the efforts of the Report and the Association as essentially the same:

> While the Report itself added little that was new to the strategies developed by the Association over the previous couple of decades, it systematized and concretized those strategies into a single developed statement and, in so doing, provided a discursive seal between the Board of Education as a formal state institution and the 'anti-institutional' English Association. Once this had been achieved, little was left for the Association to do.[21]

It is precisely the idea of liberal-humane education which is a point of departure for Leavis's sketch for an English school at the University in his *Education and the University* (1943). Like the authors of the Report he too argues that literary studies are ideally suited to serve the cause of liberal education in "bringing the various kinds of specialist knowledge and training into effective relation with informed general intelligence, humane culture, social conscience and political will."[22] Leavis wants to make the "English School" the centre for "a real humane focus" because he believes that a study of the literature and language of one's own country is the most intimate kind of study of tradition. Leavis also points to the unique status of literary studies in their ability to "lead constantly outside themselves." As an English teacher and a literary critic Leavis wished to inculcate in his students "a discipline of scrupulous sensitiveness of response to delicate organization of feeling, sensation and imagery"[23] in their study of literature to enable them to reflect on the developments in the world outside. This reminds us of the following words from the Newbolt Report:

> . . . so poets, philosophers, and historians have the power of revealing new values, relations of thought, feeling, and act, by which the dull and superficial sight of the multitude is illuminated and helped to penetrate in the direction of reality.[24]

It may be relevant to point out here that Leavis's attitude towards the "multitude" is sympathetic because of his own middle class background and is therefore significantly different from that of the authors of the Report.

It is in place here to remind ourselves of Leavis's views on the scientific study of language. Linguisticians, he says, postpone dealing at all with meaning. Thought about language on the other hand, he says, "should entail the full and firm recognition that words 'mean' because individual human beings have meant the meaning, and that there is no meaning unless individual beings can meet in it."[25] Advocating that the scientific study of formal grammar and philology be kept apart from the study of literature, the writers of the Newbolt Report opine that "*in dealing with literature, the voy-*

*age of the mind* should be broken as little as possible by the examination of obstacles and the analysis of the element on which the explorer is floating"[26] (emphasis added). Literature is thus seen as "the voyage of the mind" and the role of the teacher is to introduce the student "to the intimacy of a greater intellect."[27] Leavis's own ideas of literature come very close to this notion as can be gathered from the following lines from a much later lecture (1969):

> It's [the poem is] "there" only when it's realized in separate minds, and it's not merely private. It's something in which minds can meet, and our business is to establish the poem and meet in it.[28]

What Leavis says here about the poem is equally applicable to his idea of literature as a whole. Leavis also recognizes literature, not only as a place where minds meet, but goes further to find a place for the teacher-critic. Thus teaching or the act of criticism helps individual student-readers to "realize" the work of art in their "separate minds."

In this light we may look more closely at the conception of the teacher in the Newbolt Report. As we have seen, the Report looks at education as providing guidance to the students in the acquiring of experience. "The intercourse of the classroom" is seen in this context as the most valuable for the student because in it "he will come under the influence of not one but two personal forces, namely, the creative power of the author whose record he is studying, and the appreciative judgment of the teacher who is introducing him to the intimacy of a greater intellect."[29] Hence the Report lays great emphasis on the training of the teacher who "must himself have received an education of the kind towards which he is to lead his class."[30] For this purpose it proposes "the enrolment of a fraternity of *itinerant preachers* of English literature" to "reinforce the regular *army of teachers*" to counteract "the influences which tend to bitterness and disintegration"[31] (emphasis added). The missionary zeal and the rigorousness of the programme are at once emphasized. What the authors of the Report envisage in training the teachers by "a fraternity of itinerant preachers" who would in turn train the young minds of the students is very similar to what Leavis expects from the "cultivated minority"[32] who work towards the creation of a broad readership through literary criticism.

In his early pamphlet, "Mass Civilization and Minority Culture" (1930), Leavis asserts that culture has always been in the possession of a minority who exercise intellectual control over the society. He explains the reasons for this exclusivity:

> In any period it is upon a very small minority that the discerning appreciation of art and literature depends: it is (apart from cases of the simple and familiar) only a few who are capable of unprompted, first-hand judgment. They are still a small minority, though a larger one who are capable of endorsing such first-hand judgment by genuine personal response.[33]

Leavis's "tiny minority" includes both creative writers and critics. The business of the literary critic is to recreate the experience of the artist as it is realized or grasped in the words on the printed page. When the critic offers his judgement, he invites the readers to agree or disagree with him. This is how the work of art enters the "collaborative process" and helps the "tiny minority" to come into contact with the broader readership, which may include other critics as well as ordinary readers.

In a letter to *The Times Literary Supplement*, Leavis himself makes it clear that his own published criticism "bears a close relation to my [his] work with the undergraduates."[34] For Leavis, therefore, critical practice or classroom interaction becomes a means to establish an "organic" relationship between the culturally creative elite and the educated mass.

Leavis's own idea of minority culture takes off from Matthew Arnold's *Culture and Anarchy* which Leavis quotes at the beginning of his 1930 pamphlet. Interestingly enough, for the authors of the Newbolt Report too Arnold provides the starting point. They quote Arnold's claim that culture unites classes. They wish Arnold had added that "a system of education which disunites classes cannot be held worthy of the name of a national culture."[35] They look forward to an educational system which would help to "soften," if not "obliterate" the lines of separation between different classes. It is here that they actually recognize the importance of the study of

English right from the school to the University. For the authors of the Report English education is clearly a means to bring about a sense of "national culture." Leavis, on the other hand, wishes to protect a minority culture which in turn helps in the creation of a broader readership.

The authors of the Report feel that a marked difference in the modes of speech of different classes and an unduly narrow ground on which they meet for purposes of social life are the causes for their division. To avoid this they suggest the following:

> If the teaching of the language were properly and universally provided for, the difference between educated and uneducated speech, which at present causes so much prejudice and difficulty of intercourse on both sides, would gradually disappear. . . . The old education was not similar for all, but diverse. It went far to make of us not one nation, but two, neither of which shared the associations or tastes of the other. An education fundamentally English would, we believe, at any rate bridge, if not close, this chasm of separation.[36]

Arnold himself had advocated the introduction of English to the lower and middle-class student at the elementary school level through a diffusion of culture to be brought about by "apostles of equality." The authors of the Newbolt Report quote Arnold himself:

> 'The great men of culture,' he wrote, 'are those who have had a passion for diffusing, for making prevail, for carrying from one end of society to the other, the best knowledge, the best ideas of their time. . . .'[37]

For the authors of the Report, the "great men of culture" are agents of the promotion through education of a semblance of unity. Arnold himself and Leavis later on emphasize instead the importance of the seminal role of these "great men of culture." The difference between the Report on the one hand and Arnold and Leavis on the other is one of emphasis, which comes out quite effectively in Arnold's words quoted above and Leavis's own regarding "minority culture" mentioned earlier on.

Margaret Mathieson, in her *The Preachers of Culture*, draws our attention to a few lines prior to the ones quoted above from Arnold where he expresses his belief that culture seeks "to do away with classes" and that "the men of culture are the true apostles of equality."[38] She has rightly pointed out the ambivalence between Arnold's egalitarianism and his contemptuous attitude towards the masses. She argues that Arnold's support for the retention of traditional curriculum for the public schools, Latin for older secondary pupils, and English for lower-middle-class and elementary school pupils, can only perpetuate the class differences he professes to eliminate.[39] The Newbolt Report too, as we have just seen, seems to offer an easy alternative to the sinking of class differences. Is there any evidence in the Report to suggest its real intentions as regards the question of class differences? Towards the end of their "General Introduction" to the Report, the authors have this to offer:

> *Many of the differences between the lot of one class and another are of little importance*: but the present advantage of rich over poor in our schools—the difficulty of the attempt to pass up the intellectual ladder and to attain the spiritual freedom conferred by a real education—is keenly and rightly felt as an unnecessary and unjust inequality. *Nothing would, in our belief, conduce more to the unity and harmony of the nation than a public policy directed to the provision of equal intellectual opportunities for all*, and service to this end would be doubly effective if it came voluntarily as from those who have already received their inheritance, and desire to share with the rest of their countrymen that in which their life and freedom most truly consist.[40] (Emphasis added)

The national need of the time, as is evident from the lines above, is not so much the elimination of the differences between classes, as "the unity and harmony of the nation." To achieve this end, they would not mind attempting to provide "equal intellectual opportunities for all." If Leavis's own ideas spring from the same spirit of nationalism, where would his own contribution to the cause of English studies and criticism place him? The difference between Leavis and the Newbolt Report is clearly one of emphasis. For the authors of the Newbolt Report the national concerns are of prime importance. English is just a means to provide the cementing bond among people of different classes. For Leavis, English itself is the essence, study of English literature in and through literary-critical practice. English and criticism also become synonymous with culture. When preservation of culture amounts to a study of tradition through literature, it is bound to perpetuate a minority culture. Raymond Williams sees in Leavis the culmination of this process of what he terms as equating culture with criticism, a process which Arnold had begun.[41] Williams exposes the narrowness of Leavis's concept of culture even as he agrees with Leavis to the extent that literature does have the capacity to record the "subtlest and most perishable parts of tradition":

> To put upon literature, or more accurately upon criticism, the responsibility of controlling the quality of the whole range of personal and social experience, is to expose a vital case to damaging understanding. English is properly a central matter of all education, but it is not, clearly, a whole education. Similarly, formal education, however humane, is not the whole of our gaining of the social experience of the past and present. In his proposals on education (in *Education and the University*) Leavis makes, very clearly, the former point, and few men have done more to extend the depth and range of literary studies, and to relate them to other interests and disciplines. But the damaging formulation of the nature of the minority remains.[42]

It is true that Leavis never conceals his ideas of "minority culture" and the dominance of the cultural elite in society in the garb of egalitarianism. In fact, his own critical practice, with its emphasis on consensus in matters of value judgement of works of art, serves to perpetuate an oligarchy of the cultivated minority, even as it tries to strengthen the national bond with its constant emphasis on the "Englishness" of the writers it deals with. Viewed from this angle, Leavis could be seen as being well entrenched in the Arnold-Newbolt tradition and in fact even strengthening it.

# NOTES

1. See Geoffrey Strickland, "The Criticism of F.R. Leavis" in *Structuralism or Criticism: Thoughts on How We Read* (Cambridge: Cambridge University Press, 1981) 147-75.
2. A reference to *The Newbolt Report* and George Sampson's English for the English, for instance, occurs in Leavis's "Mr. Eliot and Education," a rev. of *Essays Ancient and Modern* by T.S. Eliot in *Scrutiny* 5.1 (1936):84-89. *Leavis says here that conclusions "opposite to his [Eliot's] own have been come to by persons ostensibly better qualified to conclude and to pronounce," and "that he [Eliot] ought now, in common decency to read" these two books and "tell us why he disagrees"* (87; emphasis added). This can be taken as Leavis's indirect acceptance of the recommendations of the Newbolt Report. It is possible that Leavis did not want to make a more direct statement than this in view of his anti-institutional stance all through his career.
3. Margaret Mathieson in her *Preachers of Culture: A Study of English and Its Teachers* (London: George Allen & Unwin Ltd., 1975) 122-42 sees how both these sought to combat the force of the Classicists by emphasizing the moral values of science and English, the same reasons for which the Classics themselves were recommended.
4. This of course inevitably creates at least a two-tier structure and goes against the ostensible purpose of the inculcation of culture which "seeks to do away with classes."
5. Brian Doyle, "Invention of English," *Englishness: Politics and Culture 1880-1920*, ed. Robert Colls and Philip Dodd (London: Croom Helm, 1986) 90.
6. Doyle quotes the circular of the Board 97.
7. Doyle 103.
8. Doyle 104.
9. Doyle 104.
10. Doyle 104-05.
11. Margaret Mathieson, *The Preachers of Culture*, 70 quotes from G. Greenbaum, *Social Change and the Schools* (London: Routledge, 1967).
12. F.L. Lucas quotes from Terence Hawkes, "The Institutionalization of Literature: The University," in *Encyclopedia of Literature and Criticism*, ed. Martin Coyle et al. (London: Routledge, 1990) 930.

13. *The Teaching of English in England* (London: HMSO, 1921) 1.
14. *Teaching* 1.
15. *Teaching* 10.
16. *Teaching* 14.
17. *Teaching* 12.
18. *Teaching* 13.
19. *Teaching* 13-14.
20. *Teaching* 18-19.
21. Doyle 110.
22. F.R. Leavis, *Education and the University: A Sketch for an 'English School'* (1943; London: Chatto & Windus, 1972) 24.
23. Leavis, *Education* 38.
24. *Teaching* 17.
25. Leavis, The Living Principle: 'English' As a Discipline of Thought (London: Chatto & Windus, 1977) 58.
26. *Teaching* 11.
27. *Teaching* 8.
28. Leavis, *English Literature in Our Time and the University: Clark Lectures 1967* (London: Chatto & Windus, 1969) 48.
29. *Teaching* 8.
30. *Teaching* 24.
31. *Teaching* 25.
32. The "itinerant preachers" of the Report and Leavis's cultural minority remind one of Arnold's "apostles of culture."
33. Leavis, *Education* 143.
34. Leavis, *Letters in Criticism*, ed. John Tasker (London: Chatto & Windus, 1974) 148.
35. *Teaching* 6.
36. *Teaching* 22.
37. Matthew Arnold, *Culture and Anarchy* quoted in *Teaching* 259.
38. Matthew Arnold, *Culture and Anarchy* quoted in Mathieson, *Preachers* 41-42.
39. Mathieson, *Preachers* 42-43.
40. *Teaching* 25-26.
41. Raymond Williams, *Culture and Society 1780-1950* (1961; Harmondsworth: Penguin Books, 1982) 249.
42. Williams 249.

# Chapter 3

# Creativity and Community: Towards a Theory of Language

> Ideally, I ought perhaps (though, I repeat, I should not put my position in quite the terms Dr. Wellek ascribes to me) to be able to complete the work with a theoretical statement.
>
> (F.R. Leavis, "Literary Criticism and Philosophy," *Scrutiny*, 6.1, 1937, 62)

> No one put me on to Marjorie Grene's book [*The Knower and the Known*], and when I found it in Heiffer's philosophy corner, and, reading in it here and there, realized that it was what I had long been seeking (without much hope), I wasn't supposing that the author had 'initiated a successful philosophical revolution,' and I knew nothing of any group to which she belonged. Simply, I saw she had a good mind, was a cultivated person and had written the rare book that bore helpfully on my problem—a book that could be used by me and the kind of student I was proposing to work with.
>
> (F.R. Leavis, *The Living Principle*, 1975, 61)

The early Leavis's emphatic assertion that he is an anti-philosopher and his arguments with René Wellek are quite well-known. At the same time, one cannot ignore the later Leavis's open admiration for and recommendation of the philosophical ideas of Marjorie Grene and Michael Polanyi. An attempt is made here to explore Leavis's ideas of mind and matter, "selfhood" and "identity," nisus and *ahnung*, in their relation to his ideas on thought and language, life and literature, and to bring into focus a loosely structured theory behind his statements. These ideas can be seen as the informing factors behind Leavis's views on culture, community, language and creativity. We also find here a complex set of ideas bound to one another in an "organic," i.e., in a mutual and collectivistic, relationship.

Leavis is fundamentally opposed to the ideas represented by Locke and Newton, and in fact the whole of Western philosophy founded on the Descartian world view with its emphasis on the dualism of mind and matter. Leavis says that Descartes's strict separation of mind and matter sets up other polarities like the internal and the external, the subjective and the objective, the private and the public. As against the two realms of the spiritual and the material, Leavis posits a "Third Realm"[1] which is neither completely this nor that, but belongs to and accommodates both. Leavis argues that the dualism of the subjective and the objective, when extended to the world of language, brings forth a distinction between statements of fact and statements of value. He invokes Marjorie Grene[2] who refers to Richards and Ogden who in turn differentiate the objective statements of science from the "impassioned utterances of art." Richards and Ogden view the statements of art as "pseudo-statements," a view which is unpalatable to Leavis. Leavis also opposes the dichotomy between pure statements of fact and statements of value. His contention is that this sort of division is artificial. In this context he borrows Grene's response to Russell where she argues that judgements of value are implicit even in a statement of fact. Any act of fresh knowing, according to her, involves a comparison with what is already known. This inevitably brings in a set of standards and personal responses. However, the personal response itself is not entirely personal, but "a product of immemorially collaborative creativity."[3]

Fundamental to Descartian thinking is the assumption that, by reflection, one could know oneself just as one could know any external phenomenon.[4] As against this, Grene says that one does not know oneself in the way one knows the not-self. Knowing oneself is difficult because one is inside time. This also implies that one is also shaped by the past. Polanyi says that the past experience acts as tacit and subsidiary knowledge which one brings to bear on the present. Therefore, one cannot be a passive observer of reality, but is implicated in its shaping. As knowing is a temporal activity, which is always in the process of making, it can never be absolute. There is always in the act of knowing, what Polanyi calls, a "protensive pull from the future."

Equally basic to Leavis's thinking is his view of the role of language in the creation of the world, a view he shares with Polanyi and Grene. The external world becomes meaningful only insofar as we have language. It is language which helps us notice our environment and the noticing takes place within a framework of values which we share with others. The creation of reality therefore is a co-operative venture which is value-dominated.

This idea of collaboration is implicit in the creation of what Grene calls the "human world." She says that when a child is born, it instantly enters into a "world shaped by all kinds of human value-judgments."[5] The child thus belongs to the total community, which includes the actually enumerable community around it as well as a wider community which is a result of its participation in a living culture of centuries of human experience.

Language too is a result of collaborative human creativity. Grene says: "It [language] is concretely 'there' only as I utter the words and phrases chosen by the meaning (*in* me, but outward bound) which they convey and you take them."[6] Language then exists because individuals have meant certain meanings and have been able to exchange them. In this sense language becomes at the same time both subjective and objective.

The objective way of understanding language helps us reflect on the Wittgensteinian conception of language. Leavis observes that Wittgenstein himself was pretty "naive" about language, even as he was aware of the inadequacy of the linguisticians' study of language divorcing it from its meaning. The naivety represented by his conception, Leavis says, is "inimical to thought."[7] Therefore, Leavis is opposed to the idea of English students being made to study Wittgenstein. He recommends instead Polanyi, particularly his essay "Sense-Giving and Sense-Reading," an essay that concerns itself with meaning. Leavis says that while the other linguistic philosophers "slight" meaning, considering it too basic, Wittgensteinians feel that such "unconsciousness" about language "produces gratuitous logic, linguistic fatuity, unprofitable conclusion and intellectual frustration."[8] As a "remarkable linguist" (Leavis's own description), Wittgenstein is interested in the "analogical structure" of a poem, whereas Leavis is concerned with the fullest use of language and its potential to capture "original exploratory thought."[9] For Leavis, this potential is related to the force of the intention of the speaker.[10] Here Leavis also elaborates on the collaborative nature of language. The speaker's intention, he says, is completed only by the presence of another person responding to it. He asserts that there is no meaning unless individual beings can meet in a language.[11] Hence his opposition to the Wittgensteinian idea of analogies and the use of such terms as "logical space" and "areas of discourse" which to him ultimately demonstrate the limits of language. Language, in this sense of "insulating boundaries between various modes of thought" is antithetical to the collaborative and creative use of language.[12]

The same principle of mutual collaborative creation informs literature. For Leavis, a poem is "a product, and in any experienced actual existence, a phenomenon, of human creativity, the essentially collaborative nature of which it exemplifies in diverse distinguishable modes."[13] He says that it is neither private nor public, but belongs to the "Third Realm." Speaking on the importance of Grene to Leavis, Anne Samson says:

> . . . that they [Grene's ideas] carry the implication that the thought proper to the creative writer and therefore, in Leavis's acceptation, to English Studies itself, is not a specialized mode of apprehension; rather, there is but one mode, and what distinguishes the great writer is the capacity to use that mode to the full. The collaborative interchange that establishes the poem, that establishes it as a value, is typical of all exchanges, for as Grene describes it, in the human world values are constitutive of facts, and values are instituted by the community. Our world, all our world is the product of creative collaboration. It is a world constituted by language, into which we are born, and it is only within the prior agreement of our language that we are able to disagree. This language which stretches back in time is a macrocosm of that tacit knowledge which each of us possesses (and part of our tacit

> knowledge is our language), the condition of our potentiality, Polanyi's 'protensive pull.' We are all, then, participators in creativity, and the role of the great writers is to make us conscious of this, to make us conscious of our humanity, which is our language.[14]

If a poem is a product of collaboration, then an analysis of the poem too is simply a recreation of that experience by critics with their individual responses to the marks on the page. Analysis, in other words, is in a sense an acceptance that the poem stands between those who respond to it. The poem actually takes shape when minds meet in either agreement or disagreement of what it means. Leavis says:

> My critical judgment is mine, in the sense that I can't take over anyone else's (if I did, it would cease to be a judgment). But it is not merely and possessively 'mine'; my implicit assumption being that it is right, 'I know that it is not mine'—and that my responsibility is to mean it as universally valid.[15]

Blake's pronouncement "I know it is not mine," which describes his creative work is employed here by Leavis to indicate his own critical process. It is in this sense that the critical process becomes almost synonymous with the creative activity. Leavis's view of literature and criticism, of the interaction between the artist or critic with the community of artists or critics of the past and the present, echoes Grene's idea of the child and its environment. It may be recalled here how Oscar Wilde brings the creative and the critical faculties together in his critically creative dialogue "The Critic as Artist." He asserts: "All fine imaginative work is self-conscious. . . . Believe me, Ernest, there is no fine art without self-consciousness, and self-consciousness and the critical are one."[16] However, Wilde proceeds to argue for an independent status for criticism, even as he attempts simultaneously to exemplify the artificiality of a division between the two activities. The independent status Wilde accords to art (which would include both the creative and critical faculties) goes well with his claim that it is life which imitates art. In Leavis, on the other hand, criticism does not attain an independent status.

Rather, the creative and the critical come into existence for him in a similar fashion with the individual artist and the critic having to depend on the wider community for their existence.

It is in place at this point to consider how the idea of this akinness of the creative and critical activities is revised by the poststructuralist critics like Harold Bloom and J. Hillis Miller. True, both Leavis and the poststructuralist critics accord the faculty of creativity to the critic. But Bloom and Miller differ from Leavis in the way they perceive the nature of creativity. For the critic in the Leavisian scheme, the poem or the novel (the words on the printed page, to be more precise) is the starting point and he/she would at best be reading the author's mind giving free vent to his/her individual creativity. Bloom and Miller, on the other hand, invest critics with a degree of freedom that helps them to read texts, which in turn lead them to other texts in an endless web of interlacing relationships, with the result that interpretation of the author's mind or even ultimate judgement of the work becomes minimal. Wendell V. Harris explains how the earlier drive to establish "mastery" of texts (he is primarily thinking of the New Critics here) is replaced by the poststructuralist "indeterminacy."[17] He refers to Geoffrey Hartman's term, "Revisionist Reversal" to describe their kind of creativity. Hartman in his *Criticism in the Wilderness* makes an interesting connection between the New Critics's "anti-self consciousness" and Leavis's own refusal to theorize.[18] This makes us wonder if the difference between Leavis and the poststructuralists could be traced to their opposing views on language and its referentiality. While in Leavis a word would refer to something other than itself, for the poststructuralists it seems only to be self-referential. Miller considers the notion of a referential use of language an illusion. He prefers to see the human condition instead in a complicated web of metaphorical analogies going back to centuries.[19] Also, he and the other poststructuralists do not seem to offer any method of criticism. In fact, Bloom does not even bother whether any other critic would share his own "vocabularies of revisionary ratios, of crossings, of whatever."[20] Leavis's attempt, on the other hand, has been to arrive at a consensus arising out of a group of practising critics.

This brings us to a consideration of Leavis's idea of the self as a real, intersubjective subject, an idea he shares with Grene and Polanyi, in contrast to the Foucauldian idea of the self or subject as a mere discourse traversed by other discourses. Foucault sees the author function, for instance, as the manifestation of "the appearance of a certain discursive set" amidst the circulation, and functioning of certain other discourses.[21] The emergence of the real self or the subject in a sense is thus overshadowed by the overpowering and constricting quality of language in any discourse. As against this, Leavis's idea of the self, being simultaneously conditioned by language (which is already constituted by an intersubjective circulation of selves) as well as contributing to it, is definitely more progressive, at least in theory. Now to go back to a consideration of Leavis's ideas on the individual and the society. In this context Leavis brings in Polanyi who says that "mind" is there only in individual human beings and that an individual mind belongs to a person who has a body and a history. The individual's response is therefore to a certain extent influenced by them. He says: "His mind is the mind of his body, and his body is the body of his mind. The dualism that has defeated so many epistemologies is eliminated here."[22] The importance Polanyi accords to history is very similar to Leavis's insistence on tradition and cultural continuity.

It is the presence of the individual human being in the whole act of knowing that takes us to the significance in the Leavisian critical terminology of "life." He says:

> When . . . I wrote 'Life *is* a necessary word,' I also wrote that life is 'there' only in individual beings, meaning that the only way in which one can point to life as concretely 'there' is to point to an individual being and say, 'There you have an actual manifestation of life.'[23]

Leavis's opposition to the "technologico-Benthamite" civilization of his day springs from its negation of this "living principle." The Descartian world-view and the technological civilization, in Leavis's view, represent this negation of life. The only way to counter them, Leavis feels, is to assert the principle of life. Here lies the responsibility of literary criticism, the English School and the University. Leavis lays down clearly the task before him. He wants to create a centre of the educated public where there

> . . . must be practised thinking that brings in consciously, pertinacious and delicate resource, the un-Cartesian reality underlying language and implicit in it; what is inexpressible in terms of logic and clarity, the unstatable, must not be excluded from thought . . . .[24]

What the assertion of life means to Leavis can be understood from his appreciation of Blake, Dickens and Lawrence. Blake represents for him an anti-Newtonian-Lockean view of life. In his discussion of Blake he formulates a distinction between the terms selfhood and identity:

> 'Identity' is Blake's word. He uses it in relation to 'selfhood,' its antithesis. The individual as 'selfhood' wills egotistically, from his own enclosed centre, and is implicitly intent on asserting possession. As creative identity the individual is the agent of life, and 'knows he does not belong to himself.' He serves something that is quite other than his selfhood, which is blind and blank to it.[25]

He finds Dickens too making the same kind of distinction. Leavis goes on:

> The selfhood asserts its rights, and possesses, from within its egocentric self-enclosure; the identity is the individual being as the focus of life—life as heuristic energy, creativity, and, from the human person's point of view, disinterestedness. It is impossible to doubt that Dickens, like Blake, saw the creativity of the artist as continuous with the general human creativity that, having created the human world we live in, keeps it renewed and real. This day-to-day work of collaborative creation includes the creating of language, without which there couldn't have been a human world.[26]

What Leavis means by selfhood may be similar to the subjective realm in the Cartesian framework. Leavis may have also been reacting against the Romantic exaltation of the self and self-expression. As against this, Blake posits identity, which offsets the subjective point of view by relating itself to the "general human creativity." In this context it is pertinent to talk about the theories of impersonality of Leavis and Eliot.[27] Leavis himself contrasts Eliot's work with that of Blake. For Eliot, a work of art springs from the writer's ability to transcend the limitations of the self by a recognition of the man who suffers and the mind that creates. Leavis, on the other hand, sees an artistic creation as springing from "the pressure of living." That Eliot has substantially modified his idea of impersonality by 1940 in his Yeats Lecture needs to be stressed at this point. Eliot describes his earlier notion as expressing only an "adolescent grasp of that idea" and that "[t]here are two forms of impersonality; one that which is natural to the mere skilful craftsman, and that which is more and more achieved by the maturing artist."[28] While the first kind of impersonality results at best only in an "anthology piece," devoid of the "particularity" needed for the expression of a general truth, the second kind, arising out of an "intense and personal experience" succeeds in expressing it. He finds a "visible development" in Yeats's poems after 1904 towards this mature impersonality. Leavis's refusal to take cognizance of Eliot's modification is related to his admiration of Lawrence (which in turn is linked with the exchange of words between Eliot and Lawrence) and Leavis's own Non-Conformist views which clash with Eliot's proclaimed Anglo Catholicism. Bernard Bergonzi[29] details Leavis's "long road to rejection" culminating in his dismissal of Eliot's doctrine of impersonality in 1958—years after Eliot's modification of his own views—even as he continues to cling on to Eliot's view of tradition and the poet's relation to the past. Bergonzi too sees this as arising from Leavis's allegiance to Lawrence and the value Leavis attaches to individual creativity. Bergonzi, and Bilan before him, have rightly pointed out that Leavis continues to use the criteria of impersonality to judge the greatness of George Eliot and that he even quotes Eliot's "Tradition and Individual Talent," the very essay he finds fault with in 1958. Bergonzi also refers to Leavis's disapproval of the Christian orthodoxy of Eliot's *After Strange Gods*. According to Leavis it is this orthodoxy which had a debilitating effect on Eliot's criticism. At the same time, Leavis approves of Eliot's belief in tradition and continuity. For Leavis then, the artist's intense personal experience has a definite role in the creative process. However, it is not like the Romantic notion of "spontaneous creation" either. This is made clear in a statement like "[a]s individuals, we are life, which transcends us."[30] Leavis thus emphasizes the individual's own contribution to life which transcends him/her. The interaction between the individual and the community he/she lives in is suggested here. Leavis says that what is true of Blake is also true of all great writers:

> The thinking of all great writers, the representatively human quality of genius being inseparable from its intense individuality, is distinctive, involving in each case a marked distinctiveness in the report on reality that is conveyed.[31]

The "distinctive" response postulated in the above lines is to be one informed by "the intuited 'living principle'—the principle implicit in the interplay between the living language and the creativity of individual genius."[32] The inseparability of selfhood and identity in their relationship to "life" is best brought out by Leavis in the following words:

> The 'identity' and the 'selfhood' are not separable, but present in the organic wholeness of every human life a varying relation—or perhaps it would be better to say a shifting emphasis on one or the other.[33]

Related to the notion of selfhood and identity in Leavis are the terms nisus and *ahnung*, though he is rather vague in his explanation of these terms. However, it can be gathered that nisus refers to an artist's individual creative effort while *ahnung* may refer to an "inkling" (Lawrence's term), "anticipatory apprehension," "foreboding," or "a pull from the future necessary for knowing" (Grene's terms). Polanyi, according to Leavis, feels that the drive to even a scientific discovery comes from a "'faculty for integrating signs of potentialities, a faculty that we may call the power of *anticipatory intuition*.'"[34] Leavis shows how Polanyi, in the following lines from *Knowing and Being*, relates this power to imagination:

> Poincare emphasizes that illumination does not come without

> the previous work of the imagination. This applies also to what I call intuition. A problem for inquiry comes to the scientist in response to his roaming vision of yet undiscovered possibilities. Having chosen a problem, he thrusts his imagination forward in search of clues and the material he thus digs up—whether by speculation or experiment—is integrated by intuition into new surmises, and so the inquiry goes on to the end.[35]

Explaining the notion of creativity in science as well as the imaginative arts later in *The Living Principle*, Leavis says:

> The scientific discoverer, Polanyi points out, adducing the evidence, has an apprehension of a pattern asking to be verified (and that is, discovered) in the field of his special interest and frequentation. That gives a direction to a sustained activity of experimental research. In the course of this the intuition, if at all near the mark, will be confirmed, and confirmation will involve refinement and development. Polanyi associates 'intuition' with 'imagination.' I myself . . . use the word *ahnung* by way of emphasizing . . . that imagination, like intuition, is concerned with the real and that the establishing of the given reality by the seeker on the frontiers of the known lies now (he hopes) in the not too remote future.[36]

Leavis draws on Lawrence to give a definite shape to this notion and he quotes him from his "Introduction to These Paintings":

> Any creative act occupies the whole consciousness of a man. This is true of the great discoveries of science as well as of art. The truly great discoveries of science and real works of art are made by the whole consciousness of man working together in unison and oneness: instinct, intuition, mind, intellect all fused into one complete consciousness, and grasping what we may call a complete truth, or a complete vision, a complete revelation in sound.[37]

Leavis also says that *ahnung*, this "clumsy phrase," involves a belief in human creativity and our conception of time. Reflecting on a passage about the act of knowing and understanding from Grene's *The Knower and the Known*, Leavis says that it is

> . . . concerned explicitly with the mode of life's asserting itself, developing into humanity, and creating—as it continually recreates—the 'human world.' The 'pull from the future,' as the brief passage recognizes, is at the same time 'anticipatory apprehension,' for knowing itself is achievement; *ahnung* goes with 'nisus'—terms for which the 'laws of inanimate nature' have no use.[38]

Leavis emphasizes here Grene's contention that in the act of knowing, the end in sight, even when only guessed at, draws us towards a solution. Therefore, for understanding to result, the individual's "anticipatory apprehension" along with "the pull from the future" has to be combined with individual effort. Language itself, for Leavis, is a result of this process. Talking about language he says:

> It takes the individual being, the particularizing actuality of life, back to the dawn of human consciousness, and beyond, and does this in fostering the *ahnung* in him of what is not yet—the as yet unrealized, the achieved discovery of which demands creative effort.[39]

It is clear now that Marjorie Grene's conception of knowledge represents a synthesis of the dichotomy of the mind and body, a dichotomy Descartes would like to emphasize. Her synthesis in terms of literature would mean unification of sensibility. Leavis also contends that the whole technological mode of thought of modern society springs from the Descartian world-view. The criteria of absolute logic, clarity and distinctness devoid of the personal element also result from this mechanistic view. Leavis locates the beginnings of this kind of thinking in English Literature in the founding of the Royal Society.

Now for a brief consideration of this dissociation. In his essay "The Metaphysical Poets" Eliot finds "a direct sensuous apprehension of thought, or a recreation of thought into feeling" among poets prior to the seventeenth century.[40] The dissociation between thought and feeling that sets in around the late seventeenth century widens by the time of Tennyson and Browning, and thereafter the writers are unable to "feel their thought." He identifies here the beginnings of this change:

> In the seventeenth century a dissociation of sensibility set in, from which we have never recovered; and this dissociation, as is natural, was aggravated by the influence of the two most powerful poets of the century, Milton and Dryden.[41]

He says that while it is true that the language has become more "refined" under the influence of Milton and Dryden, the feeling has increasingly become "crude." Leavis discusses the dissociation in his essay "English Poetry in the Seventeenth Century." To him, "dissociation of sensibility" covers the development of a verse which appeals only to the public or social ear. He, in fact, refers to Eliot and concurs with his ascribing the dissociation largely to the influence of Dryden and Milton. He goes on to say:

> A serious attempt to account for the 'dissociation of sensibility' would turn into a discussion of the great change that came over English civilization in the seventeenth century—the change notably manifested in the decisive appearance of modern English prose during the early years of the Restoration. Social, economic and political history, the Royal Society, Hobbes, intellectual and cultural history in general—a great and complex variety of considerations would be involved.[42]

Now we can see how Leavis relates the virtues of prose and reason divorced from feeling, that arise in the seventeenth century, to the Descartian world-view. We can also gather that Eliot's theory of the dissociation of sensibility, with its emphasis on the divorce of thought and emotion, becomes a formative influence on Leavis's idea of the loss of organic community.[43] His discussion of the romantic poets, in which he makes extensive use of terms like "thought" and "emotion" and the arguments presented to judge the authors are very similar to those in Eliot. What are the ultimate effects of the loss of the organic community?

Leavis belongs, in fact, to a long tradition of socio-political and literary critical thought which presents more or less similar images of the loss of organic communities and their ultimate effects on the State and the health of society at large.

Edmund Burke is an early proponent of this tradition.[44] An ardent supporter of England's constitutional monarchy, he disapproved of the revolution in France. He says that the English constitutional system works after the pattern of Nature, by which they receive, hold and transmit their government and their privileges. It is placed "in a just correspondence and symmetry with the order of the world. . . ."[45] It acts like a permanent body made of transitory parts and is ". . . in a condition of unchangeable constancy, move[ing] on through the varied tenor of perpetual decay, fall, renovation, and progression."[46] The metaphor of an organism is implicit in the above lines. Burke responds thus to the seventeenth century social thought which focused upon contractual and legal relations between parts of a society. Burke argues for the perpetuation of the "natural" orders of the State as well as the Church.

Coleridge, writing in the context of increasing interest in science, believes that the condition of a society is a direct reflection of the prevailing philosophy of the age.[47] He says that the governing classes should be re-educated if men are not to be treated as mere things, and that society is not to be regarded as an intricate mechanism. Coleridge regards the State as the protector of individuals' property. He also envisages greater role for the Church in the education of the masses and the re-education of the governing classes. In any State he sees two forces operating—those of permanence, which he identifies with the landed interest and those working for progression, represented by the commercial interest. It is the duty of the National Church, the third estate of the realm, to mediate between these two forces. His National Church or the clerisy is made up of a small number of intellectuals whose duty it is "to preserve the stores, to guard the treasures, of past civilization, and thus to bind the present to the past; to perfect and add to the same, and thus to connect the present with the future; but especially to diffuse through the whole community, and to every native entitled to its laws and rights, that quantity and quality of knowledge which was indispensable both for the understanding of those rights, and for the performance of the duties correspondent . . . ."[48]

Auguste Comte, the French Positivist philosopher, distinguishes "order" from "progress" in the context of what he calls Social Dynamics, the study of changing levels of civilization.[49] "Order" exists, for him, in a society where there is stability in the fundamental principles governing it and when all its members hold similar opinions. Such a society, he believes, existed in the Catholic period. In contrast to the idea of "order" is the idea of "progress." He identifies it with the period of the rise of Protestantism and the French Revolution, a period characterized by the progress of the sciences and the failure of theology to serve as a basis for shared opinions. Comte advocates a reconciliation of "order" with the forces of "progress" to ensure stability of society. Towards this end, he proposes the replacement of the Catholic priesthood with a "scientific industrial elite" which would also meet the requirements of the industrial society.

In Germany, Ferdinand Tonnies, a sociologist, distinguishes the terms "community" and "society" in his book *Gemeinschaft and Gesellschaft* (1887).[50] *Gemeinschaft* refers to a community in which social bonds are based on close personal ties of friendship and kinship, with emphasis on tradition, consensus and informality. This pattern is found in rural agricultural societies. As against this, *geselleschaft* refers to the predominance of rational will in society where individuals remain lonely and isolated. Relationship between people is contractual; values are based on trade and contractual relationships and growth of national life is marked by rational manipulation of capital and labour.

Similar responses to industrialization have been expressed by other writers in the mid-nineteenth and twentieth centuries. All these writers assert rigidly defined social hierarchies in which decision-making rests with the elite. Tocqueville feels that traditional culture is threatened by the monotonous and routine nature of an industrial society.[51] Arnold sees the necessity of the governance of the state by the middle classes to save it from the state of anarchy.[52] He hopes to transform them through education to a higher culture before they would be able to rule. He says that only the minority of "aliens" who are unaffected by the ideas and habits of their class, persons who are led by humane spirit and love of human perfection can provide the state with the authority it lacks. Ruskin feels that the aristocracy, consisting of landowners, merchants, manufacturers, scholars and artists, has to be reconstituted "to form a highly cultivated and responsible minority, a notion very similar to Coleridge's concept of a clerisy."[53] He envisages a society in which each class will be trained to perform its own unique function to make them belong to a rigid class structure. Every individual would be fully integrated as a member of that society which would be organically formed on the model of the organic communities of medieval times.

Morris too had a "utopian communist's" (E.P. Thompson's description) vision of society in which there would be no distinction between the rich and the poor, a society in which people would work and live in happy coexistence as in an organic community. In his ideal of the organic community art would cease to be the product of the few, but would become part of everybody's work. Morris wants to revive the medieval times when there was no distinction between intellectual art and popular art. Morris is thus different from his contemporaries in the romantic tradition who accorded a special role for the intellectuals, a role which would give them power in the hierarchical structure of society.

As opposed to him is Nietzsche, who is against any form of egalitarianism, and who demands a rigid hierarchical society based on a "natural order of castes." And Lawrence too, like Ruskin before him, believes in the stratification of society into a number of levels, each level performing a distinct function. Such a stratified society, he feels, will provide an organic system in which there will be no mechanical differentiation between men. As can be gathered, each of the above writers seeks to place the intellectuals as leaders in their hierarchical structures of social relations. Lawrence too is opposed to any egalitarianism in society, as he feels it would undermine the uniqueness of individuals.

T.S. Eliot and Ortega Y. Gasset, on the other hand, see the common man as a threat to modern society. They want him to be taught to know his place in society if traditional culture is not to be destroyed by barbarism. Eliot wishes to re-establish an organic community in the form of a Christian society to counteract the evils of industrialism. His ideal community of consciously and thoughtfully practising Christians could consist of people from different classes, with each class having a definite and important function in that society. He says that this group could include some of the clergy and some intellectuals. He wants the elite to be drawn from the dominant class of the period. Eliot argues that only a minority of the privileged elite can transmit and protect traditional cultural heritage. Leavis thus inherits a rich tradition of writers who invariably make references to an ideal community existing in a more or less distant past. Such references result from a nostalgia based on their general reaction to industrialization and the disintegration it has brought about. Most of the writers, while seeking to hierarchise the societal structure, explore different ways to ensure the position of power for the elite. Their views form a kind of cumulative background to Leavis's own concept of organic community.

Leavis's immediate sources, however, are George Sturt's *The Wheelwright's Shop* and *Change in the Village*. They are particularly impressed by Sturt's description of the adaptation of every part of the waggon, which reflects the natural and spontaneous order of the life of the people in the organic community. Sturt points out how the knowledge of the wheelwrights rests in the folk collectively:

> But where begin to describe so efficient an organism, in which all the parts interacted until it is hard to say which was modified first, to meet which other. . . . I only know that in these and a hundred details every well-built farm-waggon (of whatever variety) was like an organism, reflecting in every curve and dimension some special need of its country-side, or, perhaps, some special difficulty attending the wheelwrights with the local timber.[54]

Drawing heavily on Sturt, Leavis and Thompson emphasize the loss of the "organic community" of rural, agricultural England and its slow replacement by an urban, industrialized and organized modern state. Sturt himself brings out the distinction between the "organic" and the "organized" states in the following words:

> Yet, in point of fact, they [the sawyers], you found, were spe-

> cialists of no mean order when it came to the problem of getting a heavy tree—half a ton or so of timber—on a saw-pit and splitting it longitudinally into specified thickness, no more and no less. What though the individuals looked stupid? That lore of the English tribes as it was embodied in them was not stupid any more than an animal's shape is stupid. It was an *organic* thing, very different from the *organized* effects of commerce.[55] (Emphasis added)

What characterized the organic community was a community awareness and a certain sharing of common interests, goals and beliefs. It represented a "positive culture" in which there was as yet no separation between the sophisticated and the popular levels of culture. The great agent of change was, of course, the machine, which implied mass-production, standardization and the consequent levelling-down of standards. For Leavis and Thompson the mechanized way of life had its own consequences for literature. It was no longer possible for great works of art to appeal at different levels of response, due to the increasing gap between various levels of culture and due to the failure of language as a common mode of communication. As an alternative to the organic community which is irretrievably lost, Leavis and Thompson propose building up a "civilized community" through a conscious and concerted effort. Leavis devises a programme of education (outlined in *Education and the University*) to make the citizens aware of the forces changing their environment and to develop in them an ability to "discriminate and resist." He proposes to train them to resist both the evil effects of and the sense of alienation from the environment. He believes that the only way to counteract the effects of the machine is to profit by the experience of the past.

Leavis and Thompson invoke I.A. Richards[56] who maintained that the other vehicles of tradition like the family and community having dissolved, one has to rely more on language. But, since language itself is debased by contemporary use, the burden of the upkeep of the tradition falls on literature where, they believe, "the finest and subtlest use" of language is preserved. Leavis says elsewhere that "[i]t is literature that gives access to the inherited wisdom of the race, cultural continuity depending, for the most part, on literature and the literary tradition."[57] He says that we have to depend on the minority "to keep alive the subtlest and finest parts of tradition" because

> [i]n any period it is upon a very small minority that the discerning appreciation of art and literature depends: it is (apart from cases of the simple and familiar) only a few who are capable of unprompted, first-hand judgment. They are still a small minority, though a larger one, who are capable of endorsing such first-hand judgment by *genuine personal response*.[58] (Emphasis added)

Leavis also tells us how in the minority's possession "is the language, the changing idiom, upon which fine living depends. . . ."[59] Language and literature thus become synonymous with culture. Therefore, Leavis proposes a programme of a study of literature through "practical criticism"[60] which develops among the students the ability to discriminate the good from the bad. This "training of critical awareness" forms the essentials of the "English School," as outlined in the following words:

> The essential discipline of an English school is the literary-critical; it is a true discipline. . . . It trains, in a way no other discipline can, intelligence and sensibility together, cultivating sensitiveness and precision of response and a delicate integrity of intelligence—intelligence that integrates as well as analyses and must have pertinacity and staying power as well as delicacy.[61]

His aim is to produce the educated man—the man of humane culture—who will be equipped to be intelligent and responsible about the problems of contemporary civilization. Leavis believes that it is only by such a determined effort that the tradition of taste can be kept up. This will form the basis on which his "civilized community" can be built. Leavis wants the process of reconstruction to start from universities because he believes that universities are "recognized symbols of cultural tradition." He wants to make the "English School" the centre of "a real humane focus" because he believes that a study of literature and language of one's own country is the most intimate kind of study of tradition. He also points to the unique function of literature in bringing together a diversity of fields of knowledge and thought. Leavis intends to inculcate in his students "a discipline in scrupulous sensitiveness of response to delicate organizations of feeling, sensation and imagery"[62] through practical criticism. Leavis indicates how local analysis of the nuances of the language leads them to reflect on developments in the world outside.

Leavis also makes it very clear that it is the business of the English School to stress that every great writer belongs to "the one collaboratively creative continuity" and how language makes "a continued and advancing collaborative thought possible."[63] Leavis's own endeavour as a critic is to construct a canon of literary works (his "great tradition"). His attempt is to show how each of these writers contributes to the restoration of the values of the organic community.

At the same time Leavis emphasizes the individual response of the readers or critics in their analysis of works of art. It is "a genuine personal response" of the readers that takes him a step forward from "practical criticism" to "analysis" and "judgment." Distinguishing his own terms—"training of perception, judgment and analytic skill"—from what is commonly referred to as "practical criticism" popularized by Richards, Leavis says:

> There is about it nothing in the nature of 'murdering to dissect,' and suggestions that it can be anything in the nature of laboratory-method misrepresent it entirely. We can have the poem only by an inner kind of possession; it is 'there' for analysis only in so far as we are responding appropriately to the words on the page. . . . Analysis is not a dissection of something that is already and passively there. What we call analysis is, of course, a constructive or creative process. . . .
>
> As addressed to other readers *it is an appeal for corroboration*; 'the poem builds up in this way, doesn't it? this bears such-and-such a relation to that, don't you agree?' In the work of an English School this aspect of mutual check—positively,

> *of collaboration 'in the common pursuit of true judgment'*—would assert itself as a matter of course.[64] (Emphasis added)

For Leavis, analysis is the process of recreation in response to the words of a writer. Leavis captures the form of judgement in "This is so, isn't it?"—which is an attempt on his part to ask for confirmation of his judgement by other critics/readers. He is also prepared for an answer in the form of "Yes, but-" the "but" standing for "qualifications, corrections, shifts of emphasis, additions and refinements." Leavis says that it is not possible to have a final word on any work of art and that a sense of relative value emerges out of agreements and disagreements of judgements of various critics. Leavis insists that the "concurrence appealed for" in the critical exchange "must be real or it serves no critical purpose" and that there should be no "insincerity or mere politeness" on the part of participating critics.[65] The work of art, according to him, belongs therefore to the "Third Realm" which is neither public nor merely private. The existence of a work of art itself becomes a reality only insofar as those critics dissecting it have each recreated it. Displacing the poem from the words on the printed page Leavis says:

> It's 'there' only when it's realized in separate minds, and yet it's not merely private. It's something in which minds can meet, and our business is to establish the poem and meet in it. Merely private, on the one hand, and, on the other, public in the sense that it can be produced in a laboratory, or tripped over—the poem is neither: the alternatives are not exhaustive. *There is a third realm, and the poem belongs to that.*[66]
>
> (Emphasis added)

What Leavis says here of the poem is not very different from what he says of the nature of language in general. He makes this very clear in the following words in *Valuation in Criticism*:

> Language, which is nothing apart from meaning, is the product of human creativity, and therefore *meaning* is equally the product of human creativity. Unless someone means and someone else takes the meaning, there is no meaning. It fol-

> lows that 'objectivity' in an immediately recognizable sense is a product of human creativity. In creating language human beings create the world they live in.[67]

In a chapter entitled "Verbal Interaction" in his *Marxism and the Philosophy of Language*, Volosinov discusses the creation of meaning in similar terms:

> . . . the printed verbal performance engages, as it were, in ideological colloquy of large scale: it responds to something, objects to something, affirms something, anticipates possible responses and objections, seeks support, and so on.[68]

The "responses," "objections," and "affirmations" do not seem to be very different from "qualifications, corrections, shifts of emphasis, additions and refinements," which are terms used in Leavis's critical process. Volosinov also grapples with the question of where meaning resides in a verbal performance:

> . . . meaning is realized only in the process of active, responsive understanding. Meaning does not reside in the word or in the soul of the speaker or in the soul of the listener. Meaning is the *effect of interaction between speaker and listener produced via the material or a particular sound complex.*[69]

Volosinov's location of meaning in the actual interaction of the speaker and the listener also looks very similar to Leavis's concept of the third realm. While Leavis and Volosinov agree on the interaction of the individual and society in the creation of language, we should keep in mind that they differ on the question of the primacy of the one over the other, as is to be expected between a humanist and a Marxist.

Leavis is also opposed to the idea of bringing a set of norms or criteria to judge a work of art. He says that there are no "fixed standards" and that no one who understands the nature of a judgement could talk of "imposing accepted values." (In this context, it will be in place to remember Leavis's well-known quarrel with René Wellek in his "Literary Criticism and Philosophy," *Scrutiny*,

6.1 1937, 59-70.) Viewed from these angles, Leavis's idea of criticism seems to offer infinite possibilities of interpretation of a work of art. At the same time, we know Leavis's own intolerance towards other critics. How do we account for this hostility? John Lucas sees a gradual narrowing of Leavis's spirit of collaboration:

> . . . during *Scrutiny*'s formative years in the thirties, Leavis undoubtedly gathered about him a prodigiously talented group of critics and collaborators—including Harding, L.C. Knights and James Smith—who helped him to make it a literary journal of quite outstanding importance. Again, this seems to me so obviously true that the proposition does not need to be defended. But it is equally obvious that by the time *Scrutiny* came to an end, in 1953, the sense of collaboration had quite gone. . . . In the thirties the collaborative spirit had allowed for creative disagreement. (An obvious example is the sharp exchange of views between Leavis and Knights over *Measure for Measure*.) But the later 'collaborators' were in fact hard-liners. The result was that Leavis's famous critical touchstone 'this is so, isn't it,' became shortened to 'this is so.'[70]

Bilan has already identified certain places where Leavis departs clearly from his own theory:

> I realize that one could try to argue ('Yes, but') that is what Leavis says in theory but it is not what he does in practice; that with his judgments on the later James or Auden's poetry he really does think that there can be no qualifications of his view.[71]

Bilan's discussion of the nature of Leavis's criticism helps us to see how the tendency to "enforce" his judgements has been with Leavis even in his *Education and the University* days. Here is Bilan quoting from Leavis:

> In criticism, of course (one would emphasize), nothing can be proved; there can, in the nature of the case, be no laboratory-demonstration or anything like it. *Nevertheless, it is nearly al-*

> *ways possible to go further than merely asserting a judgment or inviting agreement with a general account.* Commonly one can call attention to this, that or the other detail *by way of making the nature and force of one's judgment plain.*[72]
>
> (Emphasis added)

This Bilan rightly believes is Leavis's attempt towards "enforcing judgment." Yes, a closer look at Leavis's practice of criticism makes us wonder whether his professed openness and possibilities of agreements and disagreements of judgements of value operate only within a closed community of critics who share a common code of beliefs and interests. What, precisely, then is this common code? Also, we often get confused in the Leavisian critical terminology. Is it, to take an instance, "collaboration" or "corroboration" that Leavis expects the critics to engage in, in their critical endeavour?

L.C. Knights, one of the editors and contributors of *Scrutiny* examines this question a few years after the death of Leavis in an article entitled "Remembering *Scrutiny*." As one of those who had both admired and disagreed with Leavis, perhaps he was in a better position to assess the *Scrutiny* enterprise. He says:

> Among those who admired him he was, I think, a too powerful and pervasive force. The critic, he used to say, puts his judgments in the form 'This is so, is it not?'; and he certainly hoped to provoke a 'response' to his 'challenge.' But he did not realize the moral weight that he commanded—especially in relation to young minds fresh from school—that made 'No, it is not' virtually impossible as a response to his question. Whether he wished it or not—and consciously he didn't—his judgments and atitudes were taken over by others without his talents and without his range of supporting reading. . . . There were very few of the central *Scrutiny* group who, like Harding and James Smith, had strength of mind and personality to remain genuinely independent even while admiring.[73]

It may be worthwhile to compare at this point Leavis's idea of "common pursuit" with Stanley Fish's idea of an "interpretive community."[74] For Fish, alternative ways of understanding a sentence are possible among speakers who share a common repertoire of contexts. An institutional community of speakers who share such a common repertoire of contexts and a set of beliefs can be said to form an interpretive community. In the context of such interpretive communities, meaning becomes neither wholly determined nor entirely unmarked. However, meaning does become, in a sense, community-specific or context-specific. Though Fish's idea of the community and the possibility of a common share of meanings remind us of Leavis's notion of language and the creative and critical activities, we should be wary of equating Fish with Leavis, because for Leavis language is the common preserve of the entire community, a community which includes all the speakers of the language. Leavis's community, therefore is much more broad-based. Also, we need to keep in mind here that for Leavis the individual's own response to words (the private response) is negotiated by him/her in the language which is in the community's keeping (the public realm), which in turn makes him/her enter a "Third Realm." However, it should be noted that Leavis's own efforts as an English teacher and critic are geared towards a building of this third realm which makes it possible only for those who have this unique ability to negotiate between the private and the public spheres. Also, his attempts to promote a group of critics at the centre of the entire educational and social activity would definitely lead towards the creation of a privileged power-group.

David Holbrook identifies a possible reason for the conflict of interests in Leavis, between his fight against the Cartesian dualism and the training of individuals. Emphasizing the need for developing a philosophical debate against Cartesian thinking, Holbrook says:

> But there is another task, and that is of promoting understanding—the understanding of meaning. And this is not a task which involves the training of an elite: it is a struggle in the realm of ideas, 'out there' in the public world. While the world resents an elite, it would welcome the pushing forward of the boundaries of ideas.[75]

Whether we agree with Holbrook about the emphasis he wants Leavis to lay on philosophical questions or not, he does help us understand the theory-practice mismatch in Leavis's work. Holbrook rightly states (quite unconsciously perhaps) one of the reasons for the mismatch, i.e., Leavis's enthusiasm for "the training of the elite." Holbrook's reference to "the training of the elite" offers us a clue as to how the ostensible act of "collaboration" in criticism turns out to be after all a "corroboration."

It is relevant in this context to cite the argument Ranajay Karlekar puts forward to explain the contradiction between Leavis's concept of the third realm and his attempts to create an autonomous centre to promote humane values. Karlekar argues that the insights Leavis obtained from Marjorie Grene about all knowledge existing "' . . . only within the fundamental evaluation, first of the total community . . . , and second, within this totality, of the special community whose consensus makes possible the existence of the special discipline,'" should have led Leavis to relate language to its social basis more concretely.[76] Karlekar says that Leavis only uses these insights to endorse the validity of his third realm. He clinches the issue in the following words:

> If the Third Realm is constituted by this activity, a collaborative activity that mediates between the private and public and resolves its separation, then why should it constitute a special centre; no, the centre of human and in essence social creativity?. . . . Again, in his passionate concern for totality, a great critic pressured by the historical demands of his vocation reacts against the loss of human wholeness he sees in society and seals off and guards the notion of wholeness within a special and autonomous preserve.[77]

When the third realm is thus reduced to "a special and autonomous preserve" what happens to Leavis's plan to build a civilized community in place of the lost organic community? If the cultivated minority comprises only those few who are capable of arriving at a consensus regarding judgements of value in literary works, how would it stand for the whole community? Even if we were to accept the capacity of literary education to train intelligence and sensibility among people, wouldn't Leavis's idea of a consensus in judgements heavily restrict a free play of personal responses even when there are genuine disagreements? How are we to understand Leavis's claim on behalf of the English School and the University to restore and reconstitute the culture of the community at large? Leavis does accept that the civilized community obtained through a study of literature and literary criticism is at best a substitute to the lost organic community. However, Leavis's prejudice against any large scale democratization of education and mass literacy prevents him from envisaging a more broad-based third realm. His elitist view of culture evidenced in his assertion that culture has always been in the minority keeping does not allow him to extend the rich possibilities of a free intersubjective circulation of opinions in the community.

# NOTES

1. The term third realm was also used by the German logician G. Frege (1848-1925) in his "Thought: A Logical Inquiry." Frege divides things into the material, the spiritual and the "third realm." His "third realm" contains things which are timeless as well as non-spatial. Though for Frege all the three realms are on the same level, he says that for Plato, to whom one can trace its origin, the "third realm" was the first realm containing his forms and ideas. These ideas are obtained from L.R. Lacey in G.H.R. Parkinson, ed. *An Encyclopaedia of Philosophy* (London: Routledge, 1988) 381-401.
2. The discussion of Marjorie Grene is based on her book *The Knower and the Known* and that of Polanyi on his *Knowing and Being*, as also on my own reading of both of them through *The Living Principle*.
3. F.R. Leavis, *The Living Principle: English as a Discipline of Thought* (London: Chatto & Windus, 1977) 33.
4. The ideas expressed here on Descartes, Grene and Polanyi are from Anne Samson's *F.R. Leavis* (New York: Harvester Wheatsheaf, 1992) 71-74.
5. Leavis, *The Living Principle* 37.

6. Leavis, *Living* 37.
7. Leavis, *Living* 13.
8. Leavis, *Living* 58.
9. Leavis, "Memories of Wittgenstein," *The Human World* 10 (1973): 77-78.
10. Leavis, *Living* 58.
11. Leavis, *Living* 58.
12. Leavis, *Living* 105.
13. Leavis, *Living* 36.
14. Samson 98.
15. Leavis, *Living* 46-47.
16. Oscar Wilde, "The Critic as Artist," *The Works of Oscar Wilde* (New York: P.F. Collier & Son Corporation, 1927) 556-57.
17. Wendell V. Harris, *Dictionary of Concepts in Literary Criticism and Theory* (New York: Greenwood Press,1992) 52.
18. Geoffrey H. Hartman, *Criticism in the Wilderness: The Study of Literature Today* (New Haven: Yale University Press, 1980) 7.
19. J. Hillis Miller, "Tradition and Difference," Rev. of *Natural Supernaturalism: Tradition and Revolution in Romantic Literature*, by M.H. Abrams, *Diacritics* Winter (1972): 11.
20. Harold Bloom, *Agon: Towards a Theory of Revisionism* (New York: Oxford University Press, 1982) 38.
21. See Michel Foucalt, "What is an Author?" in *The Foucault Reader*, ed. Paul Rabinow (Harmondsworth: Penguin Books, 1984) 107 and 108.
22. Leavis, *Living* 39.
23. Leavis, *Living* 42.
24. Leavis, *Living* 43.
25. Leavis, *Nor Shall My Sword: Discourses on Pluralism, Compassion and Social Hope* (London: Chatto & Windus, 1972) 172.
26. Leavis, *Living* 43-44.
27. I have also discussed Leavis's views on impersonality (with Eliot in the background) in an article entitled "Leavis's Romantic Connection: A Response," *Journal of Contemporary Thought* (1991), particularly, 101-02.
28. T.S. Eliot, "Yeats," *Selected Prose of T.S. Eliot*, ed. Frank Kermode (London: Faber and Faber, 1975) 251.
29. Bernard Bergonzi's views expressed here are obtained from his "Leavis and Eliot: The Long Road to Rejection," *Critical Quarterly* 26.1 & 2 (1984): 21-43.
30. Leavis, *Valuation in Criticism and Other Essays*, ed. G. Singh

(Cambridge: Cambridge University Press, 1986) 289.

31. Leavis, *Living* 49.
32. Leavis, *Living* 49.
33. Leavis, *Living* 185.
34. Leavis, *Nor Shall* 22.
35. Leavis quotes from Polanyi's *Knowing and Being* in his *Nor Shall* 22.
36. Leavis, *Living* 224-25.
37. Leavis, *Thought, Words and Creativity: Art and Thought in Lawrence* (New York: Oxford University Press, 1976) 47.
38. Leavis, *Living* 66.
39. Leavis, *Living* 44.
40. T.S. Eliot, "The Metaphysical Poets," *Selected Essays* (1934; London: Faber and Faber, 1966) 286.
41. Eliot, "Metaphysical Poets" 288.
42. Leavis, "English Poetry in the Seventeenth Century," *Scrutiny* 4.3 (1935): 252.
43. It is interesting to note that Karl Mannheim (1893-1947), a German Sociologist too, like Leavis, traces the dissociation ("the breaking up the wholes" is Mannheim's term) to Descartes and Hobbes and that he too uses the metaphor of the organism in his sociological analysis of the State. (For more information see Karl Mannheim, *Essays on Sociology and Social Psychology*, ed. Paul Kecskemeti, London: Routledge & Kegan Paul Ltd., 1953, particularly 165-82). Mannheim, along with Eliot, Christopher Dawson and Middleton Murry formed a group known as the "Moot." Even as Leavis shares Mannheim's ideas of the uniqueness of the individual and by extension the nation, and of the importance of the role of intuition in the act of knowing, we need to keep in mind that Leavis emphasizes the interaction of the individual and society.
44. Burke's ideas summarized here are obtained from his *The Writings and Speeches of Edmund Burke*, Vol. 3 (Boston: Little Brown Company, MDCCCCI) 275-375.
45. Burke 275.
46. Burke 275.
47. Coleridge's ideas presented here are obtained mainly from John Colmer, *Coleridge: Critic of Society* (Oxford: Clarendon Press, 1959) and John Colmer, *Coleridge to Catch-22: Images of Society* (London: Macmillan, 1978).
48. Colmer, *Coleridge to Catch-22*, 20-21.
49. Comte's ideas summarized here are taken from Bruce Mazlish,

"Comte, Auguste," *The Encyclopedia of Philosophy*, ed. Paul Edwards (New York: Macmillan & Free Press, 1972) and from Leszek Kolakowski, *Positivist Philosophy: From Hume to the Vienna Circle*, tr. Norbert Guterman (1968; Harmondsworth: Penguin Books, 1972). Though Leavis too, like Comte, believes in the restoration of the organic community in some form, it must be noted that he is *not* a positivist. In fact, Leavis is opposed to the main tenets of positivism such as, empiricism, disregard of value judgments and belief in science.

50. Tonnies' views on community and society are obtained from George Theodorson and Achilles Theodorson, eds., *A Modern Dictionary of Sociology*, 63-64 and Horace M. Miner, "Community-Society Continua," *International Encyclopedia of the Social Sciences*, ed. David L. Sills (New York: Macmillan & Free Press, 1972).
51. A Summary of the views of Tocqueville, Nietzsche and Gasset are taken from Alan Swingewood, *The Myth of Mass Culture* (London: Macmillan, 1977) 2-7.
52. The views of Arnold, Ruskin, Morris, Eliot and Lawrence presented here are taken from Lesley Johnson, *The Cultural Critics: From Matthew Arnold to Raymond Williams* (London: Routledge & Kegan Paul, 1979).
53. Lesley Johnson, 56.
54. George, Sturt, *The Wheelwright's Shop* (1923; Cambridge University Press, 1980) 66-67.
55. Sturt 33.
56. Leavis and Denys Thompson, *Culture and Environment* (London: Chatto & Windus, 1933) 81.
57. Leavis, "Why Universities?" *Scrutiny* 3.2 (1934): 126.
58. Leavis, *Education* 143.
59. Leavis, *Education* 145.
60. Leavis uses here a term popularized by Richards. How he extends the scope of "practical criticism" is dealt with later on in the chapter.
61. Leavis, *Education* 34.
62. Leavis, *Education* 38.
63. Leavis, *Living* 49.
64. Leavis, *Education* 70-71.
65. Leavis, *English Literature in Our Time and the University: Clark Lectures 1967* (London: Chatto & Windus, 1969) 47.
66. Leavis, *English Literature* 48. Leavis's third realm reminds us of Coleridge's third estate of the realm. While Coleridge's third estate

consists of a clarity of intellectuals responsible to the community as a whole, Leavis's third realm is more of an abstract idea where minds meet.

67. Leavis, *Valuation* 285.
68. V.N. Volosinov, *Marxism and the Philosophy of Language*, tr. Ladislav Matejka and I.R. Titunik (New York and London: Seminar Press, 1973) 95. By comparing Leavis with Volosinov I don't mean to suggest that Leavis knew him. But Volosinov was working around the same time as Leavis. It is more the comparison of ideas circulating around the same time that interests me. Volosinov's categorization of the two major trends in the philosophy of language as "abstract objectivism" and "individual subjectivism" is also useful in placing Leavis's conception of language. It has now been more or less established that Bakhtin sometimes wrote in the guise of Volosinov.
69. Volosinov 102-03.
70. John Lucas, "Yes, But Hang on a Minute," *Moderns & Contemporaries: Novelists, Poets, Critics* (Sussex: The Harvester Press, 1985) 154.
71. R.P. Bilan, *The Literary Criticism of F.R. Leavis* (Cambridge: Cambridge University Press, 1979) 66.
72. Bilan 71.
73. L.C. Knights, "Remembering *Scrutiny*," *The Sewanee Review* LXXXIX.4 (1981): 581.
74. Stanley Fish, "Is There a Text in This Class?" *Contemporary Criticism: An Anthology*, ed. V.S. Seturaman (Madras: Macmillan, 1989) 276-92.
75. David Holbrook, "F.R. Leavis and the Sources of Hope," *The Leavises: Recollections and Impressions*, ed. Denys Thompson (Cambridge: Cambridge University Press, 1984) 168.
76. Ranajay Karlekar, "F.R. Leavis: Specialist of Wholeness," *Jadavpur University Essays and Studies* 6 (1987): 188.
77. Karlekar 188.

# Chapter 4

## Cultural Theory in Critical Practice

> Has any reader of my book [*Revaluations*] been less aware of the essential criteria that emerge than he would have been if I had laid down such general propositions as: 'Poetry must be in serious relation to actuality, it must have a firm grasp of the actual, of the object, it must be in relation to life, it must not be cut off from direct vulgar living, it should be normally human . . . '? If, as I did, I avoided such generalities, it was not out of timidity: it was because they seemed too clumsy to be of any use. I thought I had provided something better. My whole effort was to work in terms of concrete judgments and particular analyses . . .
>
> (F.R. Leavis, "Literary Criticism and Philosophy," *Scrutiny*, 6.1, 1937, 63)

The question of language has been one of Leavis's preoccupations since his *Education and the University* (1943). He looks upon language in this book primarily as a useful conveyor of tradition and culture. He emphasizes its key role particularly at a time when other vehicles of tradition like the family and the community have disintegrated due to the evil effects of science. Language thus becomes for him almost synonymous with culture. However, he finds that ordinary language has also become debased by contemporary use. (He cites as an instance the language of the advertisements.) In such a situation he recognizes the need to rely on literature where the subtlest use of language is preserved. He says that it is "literature that gives access to the inherited wisdom of the race, cultural continuity depending, for the most part on literature and literary tradition."[1] In this sense, language, for Leavis, gets produced and reproduced (i.e., maintained) in and through a major expression of culture in the form of the best literary works. As a literary critic, his own task has been to identify, among other things, a canon of literary texts which promotes a tradition of values and cultural continuity. By the time Leavis writes *The Living Principle* his preoccupation with language becomes so overbearing that it receives a comment from Anne Samson that culture becomes for Leavis a mere trace of language, instead of his early notion of language as a trace of culture.[2]

We have seen in the previous chapter the importance Leavis accords to language in the creation of the human world, to its role in making a process of continuous and collaborative thought possible and to the role of great writers in belonging to this "collaboratively creative continuity." We have also dealt with Leavis's idea of the nature of language which is simultaneously objective and subjective and with his notion of the way in which the personal and the social merge in the creative use of language. What follows in this chapter is a consideration of some representative samples of Leavis's practical criticism of poetry and the novel from the point of view of how his ideas like that of the personal and the social merge in the creative use of language of the writers. That certain general principles are indeed involved in Leavis's criticism of various writers become very clear from Leavis's response to Grierson:

> That I myself believe there may be more than one kind of good poetry might, I think, have been gathered from that paragraph of mine which Professor Grierson then quotes, and I cannot see what excuse he has for supposing me to make Donne the model and criterion: 'The seventeenth century of Shakespeare, Donne, Middleton and Tourneur,' and, I might have added, of Ben Jonson, the Court poets and Marvell. These poets seem to me to exhibit between them a wide range of differences and to have written good poetry in a variety of manners. But all these manners have, in their different ways, a vital relation to speech, to the living language of the time.[3]

Leavis considers the seventeenth century as a key phase in the history of civilization. His revaluation of poetry thus starts with an account of English poetry in the seventeenth century. In his *Education and the University* he gives his reasons for choosing this period for a special study for all students of the English Tripos:

> It is at one end in direct and substantial continuity with the world of Dante, and it shows us at the other a world that has broken irretrievably with the medieval order and committed itself completely to the process leading directly and rapidly to what we live in now. In the course of it capitalism 'arrives,' finally overcoming the traditional resistances, so that its ethos becomes accepted as law, morality and controlling spirit in the economic realm; the age of parliamentary rule begins, as does that of economic nationalism; crucial issues in the relations between Church and State, the spiritual and the secular, religion and the individual, are decided in a spirit going against the tradition of centuries—the principle of toleration is established along with that of 'business is business'; *the notion of society as organism gives way to that of society as a joint-stock company; science launches decisively on its triumphant accelerating advance.*[4] (Emphasis added)

The values Leavis associates with the seventeenth century life and those reflected in its literature and the literature that has gone before become for him the criteria for judging the literature of the succeeding centuries. Some of these criteria are: emphasis on the talking voice, liveliness of enactment and use of the dramatic medium to exploit the strength of spoken English. These are the very qualities Leavis admires in Metaphysical poetry, especially the poetry of Donne. Leavis comments in the following lines on Donne's use of the "talking voice":

> In an age when music is for all classes an important part of daily life, when poets, along with so large a proportion of their fellow countrymen, are musicians and write their lyrics to be sung, Donne uses in complete dissociation from music a stanza-form that proclaims the union of poetry and music.[5]

With the institution of the Royal Society (1662) the emphasis in language moved from the personal to the social. The polite and the "manners" in the realm of the social gave rise in language to certain prose virtues with their emphasis on rules of grammar and logic. Leavis details the developments in the eighteenth century as follows:

> The concept of correctness (a correctness that is 'easy' and 'natural') associated with Mr. Waller's reform of our numbers is inseparable from a concept of 'Good Form.' What the turn registers is a change in civilization—a change by which, in the view of the age itself, civilization was virtually inaugurated. As a result of the social and economic changes shaped by the Civil War, a metropolitan fashionable Society, compact and politically in the ascendant, found itself in charge of standards, and extremely convinced that, in the things it cared about, there were standards, to be observed, models to be followed: it was anxious to be civilized on the best models. It differed from any conceivable modern fashionable society in being seriously interested in intellectual and literary fashions. Its leaders patronized the Royal Society as well as polite letters and the theatre. If we say that the age was one in which the code of Good Form was in intimate touch with the most serious cultural code we indicate limitations and strength at the same time. The development of sensibility represented by the new ideal of poetic refinement illustrates the point: the ease, elegance and regularity favoured belong, we feel, to the realm of manners; the diction, gesture, and deportment of the verse observe a polite social code; and the address is, as has been said already, to the 'outer ear'—to an attention that expects to dwell upon the social surface.[6]

We also understand how for Leavis the establishment of the Augustan tradition coincides with a separation between sophisticated and popular levels of culture at the end of the seventeenth century.[7] As against this, he finds "a real culture of the people" in the seventeenth century, a culture that produced masterpieces such as Bunyan's *Pilgrim's Progress*. He opines that when Augustan convention and idiom, with their social suggestion dominate, sophisticated culture cuts itself off from the traditional culture of the people. The effect of these developments has consequences for Augustan literature. In his discussion of the poets of the eighteenth century Leavis says that good poetry could be produced under such circumstances only if the "correctness" of Augustan poetry is tempered by the "complexity" and "profundity" of Metaphysical poetry. He cites Pope as a poet who possessed this rare ability:

> But all the same, working in the fashionable idiom and conventions, a poet, to achieve the profound in poetry, would have to be great indeed; and Pope's greatness, we remind ourselves, is of such a kind as to enable him to transcend his age: his profound poetry has in it an essential element of the Metaphysical (and no other poet of Pope's century so communicates with the seventeenth). . . . In Pope alone, in his time, the tradition he represents may be said to bring into poetry the full vitality of the age.[8]

Leavis also comments on the variety of tone Pope achieves from passage to passage in his *Elegy to the Memory of an Unfortunate Lady*:

> After various tones of declamation, we pass through the passage anticipating (or furnishing) an Eighteenth Century mode, associated with Collins and Gray, of conventional elegiac sentiment to the deeply moving final paragraph, in which the strong personal emotion, so firmly subdued throughout to the 'artificial' form and manner, insists more and more on its immediately personal intensity.[9]

By Blake's time the deterioration (of which Leavis has given adequate expression in the passage quoted at the beginning of this chapter) had its effect on literature. What caused this deterioration? Leavis would be quick to say—loss of organic community. The influence of Descartes and the division of the mind and body, the human being and his environment, the individual and society which sprang from the scientific thinking that proceeded from him are the immediate causes for the loss. The split had its consequences for literature and culture which created two distinct levels—the popular and the sophisticated. Leavis locates the origins of this widening rift in the seventeenth century. Leavis's consideration of this split has obvious references to Eliot's idea of the "dissociation of sensibility" as we have already discussed in the previous chapter. When Leavis admires Pope's ability to achieve a strength closely related to Marvell and Donne, while being Augustan, and discusses him in relation to the "now familiar topic, the 'dissociation of sensibility,'" it is clear that Leavis more or less assumes the validity of Eliot's idea. Leavis also refers to Eliot's having ascribed "the dissociation very largely to the influence of Dryden and Milton."[10] In the absence of the ideal conditions in which a work of art could simultaneously appeal at different levels of response, Leavis places a greater onus on the part of artists to consciously appeal to them. Pope is important for Leavis precisely because he is able to do this. The notion of the common reader is therefore seen to linger on in some writers like Pope and Johnson though not beyond them. Blake's own poetry is seen as a fight against the insulation established at the end of the seventeenth century between the recognized "polite" culture and the cultural tradition at the popular level. His is also a reaction against the virtues of good prose and the Augustan emphasis on grammar and logic. Leavis says that when excessive attention is paid to the social, as it happened in the Augustan period, it is bound to result in a movement of protest in minds that are creative. Blake's reaction comes through in some "technical achievement." It will be in place to remember that for Leavis "technical achievement" is antithetical to the creative or poetic use of language. The reversal Blake has brought about becomes counterproductive with too much stress being given to individual expression. Leavis sees the effect of this in Blake's later prophetic works which betray an absence of adequate social collaboration:

> In the absence, we may put it, of adequate social collaboration . . . his powers of attaining in achieved creation to that peculiar impersonal realm to which the work of art belongs and in which minds can meet . . . failed to develop . . .[11]

From this critical "placing" of Blake Leavis moves to a complete admiration later on in his work. Blake then represents an assertion of individuality in his fight against Locke and Newton and a reaction against an overinsistence in the eighteenth century on the social. Here is Leavis on Blake:

> But for Blake the conventional order had no interest, and conventional expression falsified or ignored what individual experience told him was the real, the true and the significant: his genius was that he saw no choice but to work out a completely and uncompromisingly individual idiom and technique.[12]

Commenting on the kind of disinterestedness Blake represents, Leavis says:

> The essential objects in its preoccupation with which his poetry exhibits such purity of interest—such disinterestedness—are not susceptible of visualization; they belong to inner experience, emotional and instinctive life, the inner life of the psyche. It is Blake's genius that, dealing with material that could be present to him only as the most intimate personal experience—the very substance of his appetites, desires, inner urgencies, fears and temptations—he can write poetry that has virtues analogous to those of the 'wiry bounding line.'[13]

Leavis's adoration for Blake reaches such heights that Blake becomes for him a representative of the life principle, whereas Eliot, his antithesis, symbolizes a negation of life. An extreme assertion of individuality in the nineteenth century ends up in the cult of art for art's sake in some romantic writers. As against this, Keats develops his art in relation to life, with his emphasis on reality, direct vulgar living and grasp on actualities. Comparing Keats's "Ode to the Nightingale" with Shelley's "To a Skylark" Leavis says:

> The rich local concreteness [of Keats] is the local manifestation of an inclusive sureness of grasp in the whole. What the detail exhibits is not merely an extraordinary intensity of realization, but also an extraordinary rightness and delicacy of

> touch; a sureness of touch that is the working of a fine organization. The Ode, that is, has the structure of a fine and complex organism: whereas *To a Skylark* is a mere poetical outpouring, its ecstatic 'intensity' being a substitute for realization in the parts and for a realized whole to which the parts might be related.[14]

It can be gathered from Leavis's comment that "concreteness" evidenced in parts of a work of art is an indication of a greater "inclusiveness" of the whole "complex organism." The part-whole relation indicated here is developed into Leavis's favourite metaphor of an organism. A reference to Coleridge's idea of organicity is not out of place here. Goodson in his book *Verbal Imagination* discusses how Richards draws on Coleridge's concept of "imagination" which promotes an active participation of the reader, and which in turn helps him/her realize the significance of the work of art which is more than the sum of its individual parts. He says that it is "imagination" which joins the separable meanings of words which are left dangling by "fancy."[15] We can see how a similar idea of organism operates in Leavis, a connection Goodson does not wish to make.[16] For Leavis the finished product of a poem is a "realized whole" with interrelated parts, and so is language itself, which comes into being in the meeting of minds. Also the poem, for Leavis, is not just words on the page. The metaphor of organism invests the words with "life." The humane or the personal element that infuses "life" into words is a major consideration for him.

Leavis also shows how the personal urgency of a poet ends up in producing great poetry as in *The Fall of Hyperion: A Vision*:

> What the strength of the influence [Dante's], the intensity of the effect, shows is how much the study was part of the discipline and self-searching with which Keats met the disasters, the blows of fate, that were making life for him overwhelmingly a matter of 'the agonies, the strife of human hearts.' The immediately personal urgency of the preoccupation with suffering and death comes out plainly in the passage describing his nightmare race against the burning of the 'gummed leaves' (II, 106-134). But this personal urgency is completely imper-

> sonalized; it has become the life, the informing spirit, of the profoundest kind of impersonality.[17]

There is a return to good poetry only in Hardy and Hopkins in the late Victorian period. For Leavis, Hopkins represents a poetry close to living speech. There is an emphasis in his poetry on current spoken idiom. Of Hopkins Leavis says:

> That he was consciously bent on bringing back into poetry the life and strength of the living, the spoken, language is explicit—the confirmation was pleasant to have, though hardly necessary—in the *Letters* (to Bridges, LXII): 'it seems to me that the poetical language of the age shd. [sic] be the current language heightened, to any degree heightened and unlike it, but not (I mean normally: passing freaks and graces are another thing) an obsolete one.'[18]

Leavis also distinguishes Hopkins's grasp of the real from that of the "Victorian-romantic" in the following words:

> The Victorian-romantic addicts of beauty and transience cherish the pang as a kind of religiose-poetic sanction for defeatism in the face of an alien actual world—a defeatism offering itself as a spiritual superiority. Hopkins embraces transience as a necessary condition of any grasp of the real. The concern for such a grasp is there in the concrete qualities that give his poetry its vitality—which, we have seen, involves an energy of intelligence.[19]

When we examine Leavis's adverse criticism of various poets across the centuries, some of the same criteria we have seen above seem to operate. For instance, Milton is dislodged from his high position on the grounds of an "extreme and consistent remoteness of Milton's medium from any English that was ever spoken."[20] After analyzing a passage from Book VI of *Paradise Lost* Leavis says:

> It needs no unusual sensitiveness to language to perceive that, in this Grand Style, the medium calls pervasively for a kind of

> attention, compels an attitude towards itself, that it is incompatible with sharp, concrete realization; just as it would seem to be, in the mind of the poet, incompatible with an interest in sensuous particularity. He exhibits a feeling for words rather than a capacity for feeling through words; we are often, in reading him, moved to comment that he is 'external' or that he 'works from the outside.'[21]

Leavis also says that Milton uses "a medium so cut off from speech—speech that belongs to the emotional and sensory texture of actual living and is in resonance with the nervous system . . ."[22] His Grand Style and his use of Latinate expressions seem to have barred Milton from the "essential expressive resources of English" he had once commanded. Leavis says that Milton shows evidence of these in the Mulciber passage of *Paradise Lost* and in *Comus*. He speaks of Milton as being in the Spenserian line in contrast to that of Shakespeare and Donne.

Dryden too is said to be a great "representative poet" and not a great poet. He is not found to have the kind of strength Pope had in being simultaneously in his time and with the Metaphysical poets. Leavis says:

> The community to which Dryden belongs as a poet is that in which he actually lives, moves and talks; and he belongs to it so completely and, with its assurance of being sophisticated and civilized (it on the point of considering itself truly Augustan—that is, as attaining and realizing afresh a kind of absolute of civilization), it is so completely engrossing that he has no ear, no spiritual antennae, for the other community. One has more conviction in calling him a great representative poet than in calling him a great poet, for he is certainly a great representative.[23]

When we see the terms "sophisticated and civilized" it is not difficult to guess what Leavis would have meant by "the other community"—the popular society or culture. Leavis concludes that the "dissociation of sensibility" has set in with the verse being written thereafter that "appeals only to the public—or, it might be better to say, social—ear."[24] Leavis also points to Dryden's admiration of Milton's magniloquence and how the eighteenth century "derive[s] its exalted public decorum of poetry from Milton (who in Gray's Pindaric odes is inseparable from Dryden)."[25] Dryden's dramatic verse too is found to be mere "descriptive eloquence." Comparing Dryden's *All for Love* with Shakespeare's *Antony and Cleopatra* Leavis says: "It is an immediately felt superiority in the life of the verse—superiority in concreteness, variety and sensitiveness—that leaves us with 'eloquence' instead of 'life' as the right word for Dryden's verse."[26] Note how Leavis distinguishes "life" in Shakespeare from "eloquence" in Dryden. "Life," in fact, becomes the most predominant criterion and a recurrent term in the whole essay. Leavis says that Shakespeare's personae "have a life corresponding to the life of the verse; the life in them, is in fact, the life of the verse."[27] Analyzing another passage from *All for Love* Leavis comments that Dryden's "emotion doesn't emerge from any given situation realized in its concrete particularity; it is stated, not presented or enacted. The explicitness is of the kind that betrays an absence of realization."[28]

The Romantic conceptions of genius and inspiration have developed, according to Leavis, as a reaction against the Augustan insistence on the social and the rational.[29] Shelley's weakness is diagnosed as his "weak grasp upon the actual,"[30] the weakness being attributed to his idealism and Platonism. He is said to offer feeling divorced from thought, even opposed to thought.[31] He is also said to offer emotion "in itself, unattached, in the void." Leavis comments: "'In itself,' 'for itself'—it is an easy shift to the pejorative implications of 'for its own sake' . . .'"[32] Leavis describes thus Shelley's inability to grasp anything, to present anything as existing in its own right. The notable exception to these qualities is his Mask of Anarchy where the "emotion seems to inhere in the vision communicated, the situation grasped. . . ."[33] "His handling of the medium," Leavis says, "assimilates him readily, as influence, to the Spenserian-Miltonic line running through Hyperion to Tennyson."[34]

Among the poets of the twentieth century, Eliot becomes the target both of admiration and of attack. Leavis seems to be quite happy with Eliot's early poetry. In "Prufrock," he sees a "poetry that expresses freely a modern sensibility, the ways of feeling, the modes of experience, of one fully alive in his own age."[35] Similarly, the utterances of the lady in his "Portrait of a Lady" are found to be "in the idiom and cadence of modern speech."[36] While he finds both these poems arising from "directly personal embarrassments, disillusions and distresses," he sees in "Gerontion" "the impersonality of great poetry."[37] *Four Quartets*, however, meets with a somewhat mixed response. Discussing the opening lines of the poem Leavis says that there is something "immediate, concrete and personal" about them. He says:

> The poet sinks back in his chair, withdrawing for a moment from what has become for us his total immersion in a personal problem, but it is not a withdrawal that lessens the immediacy. On the contrary, it intensifies the immediacy in a way that makes us feel it as an informing life that makes the paragraph organic from the beginning.[38]

The thinking quality of the poem is simultaneously impelled by a personal need and directed by an imperative personal concern.[39]

In his critical engagement with Harding's criticism of "Little Gidding" Leavis shows his disapproval of Eliot. Harding feels that in "Little Gidding" there is "the clearest expression . . . of a motive force other than repulsion"; Leavis, on the other hand, finds "the large part played in his [Eliot's] poetry in general by the motive force of repulsion."[40] Leavis goes on to discuss the aspect of time as dealt with by Eliot. While Leavis's emphasis is on "life," Eliot seems to insist on "the unreality, the unlivingness, of life in time."[41] Leavis concludes his discussion on "Burnt Norton" in the following words:

> A poet, who offering to achieve and confirm his reassuring apprehension of a really and supremely real by creative means, dismisses all but the non-temporal 'now' as 'the waste sad time stretching before and after' stultifies himself. He is committed to discrediting the creative process he undertakes to demonstrate and vindicate; positing a kind of living that is not process (for process involves change and death), he offers

> us, dazed himself and deceived by the astonishing inner duplicity or dividedness that is one aspect of his genius, an impressive effect that considered, resolves itself into a play of distractions, evasiveness and equivocation.[42]

Leavis also tells us how "form" or "pattern"—words Eliot uses in the poem, which suggest that the whole may be more than the sum of the parts—reminds us of an organism which implies life. But these words in Eliot's use of them are related to stillness, the stillness of the "still point of the turning world," that reinforce "the suggestion of an apprehended supreme reality out of time on which the world of science and common sense depends."[43]

The emphasis in Leavis's criticism of poetry, as has been seen above, is on the use of language, its concreteness, its liveliness, its personal intensity and the strength of its spoken idiom. We have also discussed how these qualities are invariably connected with "life," a term which we see pervading all through Leavis's criticism of the novel. Leavis locates "life" in the individual. Its concrete manifestation is reflected in "the spontaneous, the disinterested, the ego free and the reality-creating"[44] nature of the individual. Leavis also connects the terms "disinterestedness" and "ego-free love" to the distinction Blake makes between identity and selfhood. The individual who represents life has conquered his selfhood and attained an identity with the other. Leavis is quite emphatic in asserting that for Blake ". . . the individual is a centre of responsibility towards something that is not him-(or her-)self."[45] He also extends this principle to human creativity in general:

> To insist that the psyche, the individual life, is both of its nature creative and in its individuality inherently social is to insist that all human creativity is, in one way or another, collaborative, and that a cultural tradition, is a collaboratively sustained reality in the way exemplified by a living language—by the language of Shakespeare, of Blake and of Dickens (to adduce three highly individual and potently creative writers).[46]

It may be noted how in the above lines the collaborative-creative nature of individuals is reflected in the "living language" of great writers. We have already pointed out (in our discussion of Leavis's idea of the loss of organic community) that Leavis disapproves of any separation between the individual and society, and a living organism and its environment. For Leavis, there can be no consideration of "life" without an emphasis on individuality. At the same time, "life" with its individuality ought to be a part of and outcome of collaborated community culture. We may reiterate Leavis's words referred to in the previous chapter in this context: "As individuals, we are life, which transcends us"[47] (emphasis added). Merle Brown's study of the idea of communal creativity in Leavis is useful in this context. He describes the process of the development in Leavis's idea of the individual in relation to the community, in the following words:

> Life, as Leavis never tires of saying can be lived only by individuals. But to believe as an individual human being is to be developing as a person, to be struggling constantly to attain integrity, a continuousness between one's inward thoughts and feelings, one's outward acts and speech, and the natural and social situations in which one feels, thinks, acts and speaks. Even more important, human creativity depends upon one's developing as a self-world, a person, in such a way that he is openly expectant that he will be impinged upon by other persons.[48]

However, it is difficult to agree with Brown who says later on in the essay that Leavis's idea of the collaboration of the self and the other implicit in the above description is actually practised by Leavis in his engagement with others, considering his penchant for sticking to his own position in his arguments with many critics. Leavis feels that insofar as great art reflects life, it ought to emphasize the actual relationship of men to their environment. He emphasizes this necessity of the individual in relation to others in his criticism of the novelists in *D.H. Lawrence: Novelist* (1955):

> The insistence on the individual, or 'fulfilment' in the individual, as the essential manifestation of life carries with it a cor-

> ollary . . . it is only by way of the most delicate and complex responsive relations with others that the individual can achieve fulfilment.[49]

Leavis explains how his own ideas on "life" and the individual are related to Lawrence's own in his *Psychoanalysis and the Unconscious*. He quotes from Lawrence:

> Where the individual begins, life begins. The two are inseparable, life and individuality. And also, where the individual begins, the unconscious, which is the specific life-motive, also begins.[50]

Leavis goes on to say how these words help him connect Lawrence's ideas of "life" and "individuality" to his own questions of language:

> The emphasis falls for my own purpose on what I call the Third Realm (neither private nor, for science, public), which both my purpose and my firm certitude represent by language, in which, having created it, individuals meet, and in meeting (they meet in meaning) carry on the creative collaboration that maintains and renews what we think of as a life—i.e. the language. But this 'life' (inverted commas now—though it's a reality and a key one) couldn't exist but for the life that's 'there' only in individuals (and human individuals couldn't live without that non-computerable reality).[51]

Leavis's criticism of the novelists makes extensive use of "life" and its related terms. He elaborates Jane Austen's preoccupation with "life" in the following words:

> . . . her interest in 'composition' is not something to be put over against her interest in life; nor does she offer an 'aesthetic' value that is separable from moral significance. The principle of organization, and the principle of development, in her work is an intense moral interest of her own in life that is in the first place a preoccupation with certain problems that

> life compels on her as personal ones. She is intelligent and serious enough to be able to impersonalize her moral tensions as she strives, in her art, to become more fully conscious of them, and to learn what, in the interests of life, she ought to do with them. Without her intense moral preoccupation she wouldn't have been a great novelist.[52]

The above lines no doubt emphasize how Jane Austen transforms the personal into something impersonal; they underline the significance of "life" no less.

It is the aspect of impersonality again that predominates Leavis's appraisal of George Eliot. He says that the success of *Silas Marner* is conditioned by "the absence of personal immediacy. . . ."[53] He also says that it is

> . . . in the part of *Felix Holt* dealing with Mrs Transome that George Eliot becomes one of the great creative artists. She has not here, it will be noted, a heroine with whom she can be tempted to identify herself.[54]

Leavis's drawing upon the theory of impersonality and the "absence of personal immediacy" he finds in *Silas Marner* makes us wonder whether Leavis at this stage subscribes at all to T.S. Eliot's theory of impersonality. His moving away from Eliot's idea of a complete extinction of personality to one of an "identity" of the "self" with the society may be attributed to his subscribing to the ideas of Blake and Lawrence. In Henry James Leavis finds a different kind of impersonality. He sees James moving away from presenting either American life (as in *Roderick Hudson* and *The American*) or English manners (as in *The Awkward Age* and *What Maisie Knew*) to something international in *The Portrait of a Lady*. He says:

> We have further an intimation that, in the depths of his mind, in the interplay between the diverse actualities of his experience, there is forming an imagined ideal positive that is not to be identified with any one of them. And this brings us to *The Portrait of a Lady*.[55]

Leavis also recognizes how James's inability to find an approximation to his ideal anywhere turns him into a recluse. He offers a diagnosis of this inability in James:

> James had no such immediate sense of human solidarity [like Lawrence], no such nourishing intuition of the unity of life, as could make up to him for the deficiencies of civilized intercourse: life for him must be humane or it was nothing. There was nowhere in his work that preoccupation with ultimate sanctions which we may call religious.[56]

What Leavis is indicating by "human solidarity" or "unity of life" may be a positive attitude on the part of an artist to come to terms with the society. Leavis's disapproval of the later James could be related to his ideas on the necessity of the artist to be rooted in his own culture. The rootedness in an American or English culture evidenced in James's early works disappears for Leavis in his later works where James deals with the international theme. We may recall here Leavis's emphasis on Englishness which we discussed in chapter 2 of this book. Though Conrad is not English, for Leavis he becomes very much English by his nurturing:

> Conrad's English, as we read his supreme things, compels us to recognize it as that of a highly individual master, who has done his creative thinking and feeling—explored most inwardly the experience moving him to creation—in that language . . . . The point I am making is that, as a writer, he had to English the relation we think of as that of the distinguished poet. He used it to bring to definition an intensely personal sense of life, and did this with a responsiveness to the finer potentialities of language so vital and delicate that he stands among those writers whom (if we do them justice) we see as pre-eminently its maintainers.[57]

Francis Mulhern too points out Leavis's emphasis on the English tradition, especially in *The Great Tradition*:

> The story of the book [*The Great Tradition*] is the victory of

> an English tradition over the circumstances of origin and, crucially, over the latter day Renaissance, French realism. Thus, James may be located in 'a distinctively American' line, but this is as it were a ruse of tradition: Hawthorne emancipated James from the influence of Thackeray and from Flaubert, making possible an authentic, enabling connection with Eliot. Conrad did learn from 'the French masters': the stylism and exoticism of his weaker writing is derived from Chateaubriand, and *Nostromo* recalls Flaubert. Yet Conrad's work, with its 'robust vigour of melodrama,' is also 'Dickensian,' 'Elizabethan' even. And if he evinces that 'racy strength' it is because, his origins notwithstanding, his 'themes and interests' actually called for the English language rather than any other. He is 'unquestionably a constitutive part of the tradition, belonging in the full sense.'[58]

It is paradoxical that Leavis uses a variation of Eliot's idea of impersonality in identifying Conrad's ability to transcend his origins in becoming English. This gives us a clue to the ulterior motives of Leavis in emphasizing the questions of Englishness which are actually related to the national need of the moment as well as his own felt need to establish English as a discipline in the university. This also explains how it is not so much the Englishness of the writers that makes them belong to *The Great Tradition*, but it is their exemplification in some way or the other of the living principle. What strikes Leavis in Conrad too is the "life-like convincingness" of his characters. But he warns us that this does not mean that they exist for us outside the book. Here too Leavis goes to Eliot for support:

> A 'living' character is not necessarily 'true to life.' It is a person whom we can see and hear, whether he be true or false to human nature as we know it. What the creator of character needs is not so much knowledge of motives as keen sensibility; the dramatist need not understand people, but he must be exceptionally aware of them.[59]

One wonders how a "keen sensibility" and an "exceptional awareness" of an artist is in consonance with his/her not "understand[ing]" people. But Leavis sees these qualities nevertheless as strengths that had informed Elizabethan drama. This is the very strength that Leavis sees in *Nostromo* also. What Leavis intends to say by this distinction between truthfulness to life and life-like convincingness could perhaps be understood by the distinction he subscribes to between selfhood and identity. With identity the separation between the personal and the social breaks down. Therefore, real life as presented by an artist becomes the less real when it is mediated by his/her personal view. The personal-social coalescence thus becomes an operative tool in Leavis to measure the greatness of novelists. Though the organic community is lost historically, Leavis has always felt that values such as community relations could be consciously built by an intelligentsia (which includes the artists, critics and intelligent readers) in an effort to construct a civilized community in its place. The emphasis in such an endeavour inevitably falls on an intersubjective circulation of values. A major part of Leavis's discussion of writers therefore addresses itself to such collaborated community lives, imagined communities of writers at times perhaps, if not real ones. It needs to be pointed out here that it is this very intersubjective circulation of opinions that Leavis attempts to construct in his imagined critical community of the third realm.[60]

It is interesting to see how Leavis exempts *Hard Times* from his general censure of Dickens as an entertainer in his *The Great Tradition*. (It is pertinent to note that the Leavises term the chapter on *Hard Times* as "something in the nature of an appendix" to *The Great Tradition* in their Preface to *Dickens, the Novelist*, 11.) The clue to the inconsistency of his censure here, and of later appreciation resulting in his writing a full length study of Dickens with Q.D. Leavis (which has rightly bothered some critics) seems to lie in the nature of his appreciation of *Hard Times* itself. It is the "self-forgetfulness" of Sissy which is an antithesis of the "calculating self-interest" of the Gradgrind-like characters that appeals to Leavis in *Hard Times*:

> What may, perhaps, be emphasized is that Sissy stands for vitality as well as goodness—they are seen, in fact, as one; she is generous, impulsive life, finding self-fulfilment in self for-

> getfulness—all that is the antithesis of calculating self-interest. There is an essentially Laurentian suggestion about the way in which 'the dark-eyed and dark-haired' girl, contrasting with Bitzer, seemed to receive a 'deeper and more lustrous colour from the sun,' so opposing the life that is lived freely and richly from the deep instinctive and emotional springs to the thin-blooded, quasi-mechanical product of Gradgrindery.[61]

Leavis's preoccupation with "life" and the self-effacing qualities of the characters in *The Great Tradition* as a whole must have influenced him in the exception he makes at this point to Dickens's *Hard Times*.

The sense of the individual in relation to the community is the starting point of the Leavises's judgement of Dickens. In their chapter "Dickens and Blake: *Little Dorrit*" the Leavises say:

> . . . he [Dickens] knows that the serious and developed study of the individual life can't but be a study of lives in relation, and of social conditions, conventions, pressures as they affect essential life. The really great novelist can't but find himself making an evaluative inquiry into the civilization in which he finds himself—which he more and more finds himself in and of.[62]

In their analysis of *Little Dorrit* they discuss the question of the individual and his/her responsibility in relation to others as is manifest in the following:

> Doyce's indefeasible 'responsibility towards something other than himself' entails, to be effective, his being strongly conscious of it. Such a consciousness can hardly not entail a sense of one's identity's being important; one's identity is oneself, and, as the habit of this last word in free use intimates, the shift to a dominating sense of one's unique and unshared selfhood as the important thing is insidiously easy.[63]

The characters' adequate social collaboration becomes an important criterion to judge the work as it happens in the case of *Little Dorrit.* In a significant passage in which "life" is brought in relation to several other criteria that are important to Leavis, the Leavises emphasize the necessity of collaboration:

> Reality, courage, disinterestedness, truth, spontaneity, creativeness—and, summing them, life: these words, further charged with definitive value, make the appropriate marginal comment. *Little Dorrit*, whose desolate sense of the unreality is what we have been sharing, is the focal presence of what they stand for. But she is beaten. For her—a profound irony—the real is what, at her father's liberation, she left behind in Marshalsea. The point implicitly made (the book makes it in many ways) is that reality is a collaborative creation: *Little Dorrit*, in 'chartered,' mean and gloomy London, had found collaboration in the responsive human needs of her father and his other children, and in the human good-nature of the turnkeys, the Collegians and Flora—even of Mrs Clennam. But in Italy she is wholly denied it; her love for her father is reduced to expressing itself in docility to Mrs General, the arch- unreality.[64]

The Leavises opine that it is the individuals' responsibility towards life outside of themselves that constitutes true identity. They remark that this "distinctive sense of responsibility towards life" is a positive contribution of the Romantic movement. In this context they also record their departure from Eliot's idea of impersonality:

> The kind of vital strength that makes Dickens a romantic novelist and relates him to Blake is what Eliot rules out from the creative process and the 'mind of the artist' in his account of 'impersonality,' which has for essential purpose to deny that art expresses, or in any way involves, a responsibility towards life.[65]

Now it may be clear how Leavis who used to draw upon Eliot's ideas in his early writings (as explained above in the discussion of poetry and of *The Great Tradition*) has moved away from him later on. As has been pointed out already, his admiration for Lawrence and Blake and his extensive use of their ideas to strengthen his own criteria of criticism is a development which can be seen as running parallel to his rejection of Eliot later on in his work.

Leavis undertakes a discussion of Lawrence in his *D.H. Lawrence: Novelist* (1955) and *Thought, Words and Creativity* (1976). He admires Lawrence's *The Rainbow* for he finds it a "study of related individual lives."[66] He says that the "immemorial life" in the first chapter and ". . . the England represented by the canal, the colliery-town, and the advancing railway met one another and consort in a challenging paradigm."[67] In the context of his notion of the "fulfilment" of the individuals only by way of "the most delicate and responsive relations with others" (the words from Lawrence's *Psychoanalysis and the Unconscious* have been quoted earlier in the chapter) Leavis says:

> There, in the novels, the treatment of the theme, has for a major part of its implicit moral this further insistence: except between 'fulfilled' individuals—individuals, that is, who are really themselves, recognizing their separateness or otherness, and accepting the responsibility of that—there can be no personal relations that are lasting and satisfactory.[68]

It is with his adherence to Lawrence that Leavis reaches the final stage of his patricidal instinct. In his *Thought, Words and Creativity* he rejects Eliot's theory of impersonality outright as is evident from the following lines:

> In the art the felt separation between the creatively used words and the piece of living they have the function of evoking is at a minimum. One is not kept conscious of Lawrence—not kept actively aware of him as a personal voice expounding or aiming to evoke. And he, when he feels that he has got his art right, is hardly conscious of any gap. He is realizing in imagination a completely (or purely) 'significant' piece of living: yet he is himself, in his integrity as an individual being, present in the work. This is the true impersonality; it is of supreme importance to any conception of what the essential,

> fully imagined, spiritual status or stance or human reality (perhaps all three nouns are needed) might achieve. The impersonality that Eliot credits Landor or Valery with is idea and emptiness in the one case, and mere French brilliance and aplomb on the other.[69]

Leavis says that for Lawrence, the thought demanded by life which involves "mental consciousness," is not apart from the individual human being, but springs from "the spontaneous life-motive in every organism" (Lawrence's terms in *Psychoanalysis and the Unconscious*). To separate, therefore, the man who lives and the mind which creates, as Eliot does, is to misrepresent the process of creativity. Leavis finds the emphasis on the mind a legacy of science. He refers to Lawrence's reaction to this development here:

> What he [Lawrence] warns us against are the insidious dangers that attend on being mentally conscious; what he inveighs against is the misuse of the mind that makes it an enemy of life. He exposes and inveighs a great deal, because that misuse is the distinctive mark of our scientifico-industrial civilization. To the malady that results he applies diagnostically the triad, 'will, ego and idea.' The will is that of the closed ego—Blake's 'selfhood' as distinguished from the 'identity,' and the triad of terms together means the mind, the mental consciousness, offering to work life according to its ideas, which, with the mental consciousness they belong to, have been cut off from the well-head and from the centres of living power.[70]

An interesting feature of Leavis's criticism of the novel is his deliberate exclusion of some writers from his great tradition. However, in the discussion of the few novelists he excludes, we can see the same questions of the personal in operation. Whereas Joyce's *Ulysses* seems to issue from his "personal history and the pressure [of] immediately personal urgency," his *Work in Progress* does not seem to have anything in it to control the author's interest in technique and a pre- occupation with the means of expression.[71] We are reminded of Leavis's early assessment of Blake's work which reduces it to some technical accomplishment. Therefore, the personal element and the impersonating technique Leavis seems to suggest, should assist as well as control each other to produce good literature. While Leavis finds Forster's *Where Angels Fear to Tread* and *A Room with a View* "detached" and "distanced," he sees in *The Longest Journey* and *Howards End*, the possibility of their being "detached" "precluded by the author's essential interest."[72] At the same time, he faults *Passage to India* for its personal style. He is so overpowered by Eliot's impersonal theory here that his awareness of the novel's strength in the treatment of personal relations and of the liberal tradition comes into conflict with it. The fact that Leavis disapproves of Forster's uncritical acceptance of the inferior socio-cultural milieu dominated by the Bloomsbury[73] also needs to be kept in mind.

Leavis's criticism of Virginia Woolf interestingly turns to the question of "life," though he questions her very definition of life which stresses what goes on in the mind of the writers (their "private consciousness"), rather than in the world outside. Leavis says that this could lead only to a "sophisticated aestheticism."[74] He finds the same Bloomsbury milieu responsible for Woolf's failure to develop.[75]

Leavis's essay, "The Irony of Swift" written as early as 1934 calls for special treatment in our discussion of Leavis's criticism of the novelists in that in this essay the negation of the life principle becomes the chief criterion to judge Swift. In an elaborate close analysis of Swift's writings and while commenting on specific passages Leavis concludes: "We have, then, in his writings probably the most remarkable expression of negative feelings and attitudes that literature can offer—the spectacle of creative powers (the paradoxical description seems right) exhibited consistently in negation and rejection."[76] A little earlier he says:

> Hypertrophy of the sense of uncleanness, of the instinct of repulsion, is not uncommon; nor is its association with what accompanies it in Swift. What is uncommon is Swift's genius, and the paradoxical vitality with which this self-defeat of life—life turned against itself—is manifested. In the *Tale of a Tub* the defeat is also a triumph; the genius delights in its mastery, in its power to destroy, and negation is felt as self-

> assertion. It is only when time has confirmed Swift in disappointment and brought him to more intimate contemplation of physical decay that we get the Yahoos and Struldbrugs.[77]

The presence of Swift's personal problems in a statement as this cannot be missed. Also the quality of detachment is used earlier in the essay by Leavis to praise *Tale of a Tub*. Leavis "places" him finally as a great writer with "a sense of a great force" in his work, but one whose "channels of life have been blocked and perverted."[78]

Critics have paid attention to the shift in Leavis from his criticism of poetry to that of the novel. Bilan and Eagleton see the emphasis on the formal considerations in poetry giving way to questions of life in his study of the novelists. Bilan says that Leavis concentrates more on a study of the novelists as he goes on because "the novel is better suited to his social and moral concerns."[79] However, Leavis does not completely move away from the formal considerations (words on the page) in the study of the novelists. It may be relevant in this context to cite Bilan's quotation of David Lodge:

> Dr Leavis has two distinct 'images' as a critic; he is the critic of close analysis, of 'the words on the page'; and he is the 'moral' critic *par excellence*, insisting on the responsibility of literature to be 'on the side of life.' These two images are not irreconcilable—and both can be traced to some extent in everything Leavis has written. But is it not true that we think principally of his work on poetry in connection with the first image, and of his work on the novel in connection with the second? Poets (Milton, for instance) are assessed according to their awareness of the possibilities of language; novelists according to their awareness of 'the possibilities of life.'[80]

Bilan goes on to quote Leavis himself to prove how the formal and moral concerns are indistinguishable: "Is there any great novelist whose preoccupation with 'form' is not a matter of his responsibility towards a rich human interest, or complexity of interests profoundly realized?"[81] What Leavis says here of the novelists is equally applicable to the poets. Of particular interest is Bilan's perception of how Leavis's very definition of poetry undergoes a change from a concern with the handling of language in his study of poetry to an interest in life when he discusses the poet-novelists. Eagleton settles the issue by referring to the gap between theory and practice in Leavis:

> Only Leavis escapes this formalism, with his view that the complex formal unity of a work, and its 'reverent openness before life,' are facets of a single process. In practice, however, his work tends to divide between 'formal' criticism of poetry and 'moral' criticism of fiction.[82]

While what Eagleton and others say is largely true regarding Leavis's emphasis on formal consideration in his criticism of poetry and on moral considerations in his criticism of the novel, we must remember that there are occasions in his study of poetry (such as his criticism of his seventeenth century poetry or Romantic poetry or Victorian verse) when Leavis does not overlook the moral concerns. John Gross too makes a pertinent remark on the shift from Leavis's criticism of poetry to that of the novel:

> This is not just a shift from one genre to another, in my view: it involves the replacement of Eliot by Lawrence at the centre of Leavis's critical universe, which in turn, implies less emphasis on close reading. . . . This shift of emphasis led to the concentration on moral and social criticism which Leavis had already voiced early on in books like *Culture and Environment*, but which had not run in tandem with his early writing on poetry, as I see it.[83]

An examination of the samples of Leavis's practical criticism makes it clear that there is a development of his ideas on language from his emphasis on concreteness and the spoken medium (in his poetry criticism) to its almost becoming synonymous with "life" (in his novel criticism) and leading finally to some concrete theoretical formulations (in his last books). That Leavis's criticism of poetry was mostly written in the thirties, that of his novel in the forties and the theoretical formulations at the end of his career would perhaps suffice to explain the nature of the development of his ideas. It is true that despite Leavis's early attempts to consider the novel as "a dramatic poem," his criticism of the novel does move more towards considerations of "life" as he goes on. This may be seen as a development in Leavis from being a formalist (under the influence of Richards) to becoming a cultural critic (in his attempts to wrestle with Marxism, while denying the economic basis of society). However, it is not true that Leavis was not concerned with the questions of life early on in his career. His *Culture and Environment* and "Mass Civilization and Minority Culture" are sufficient examples to prove this. Our discussion of his 1934 essay on Swift also makes this abundantly clear. His involvement with criticism of poetry at this time does leave traces of its impact in the close reading of the passages from Swift.

It is also clear from our discussion of Leavis's criticism of poetry and the novel that his theory and practical criticism reinforce each other, though concrete theoretical formulations occur only towards the end of his career. Leavis's refusal to theorize explicitly when pressed by Wellek to do so, coming along with the statement that ideally he ought to be able to complete his work with a theoretical statement (quoted at the beginning of chapter 3) sounds prophetic, considering the philosophical underpinnings of *The Living Principle*. But there is a definite deliberateness about Leavis's refusal to theorize. This emphatic denial of theory and an assertion of practice can be understood in the context of Leavis's felt need to tease out the values of the organic community from his great tradition of literary works at a time when he found the absence of those very values in society. The emphasis on practical criticism also helps him to establish the discipline of English and criticism at the university which will in turn ensure the domination of the cultivated minority. Yes, Leavis does put his theory into practice in his practical criticism. Whether he puts his ideas into practice in real life, particularly in his dealing with other critics in a collaborative endeavour, is a different question altogether.

An examination of Leavis's practical criticism over the years will have to take into account the shift in emphasis in his concerns. While in his criticism of poetry the effort is to cull out the embeddedness of the "living principle" in the concreteness of words, in his novel criticism the preoccupation is with the "amount of life . . . gone into the making" of the novel (to use Henry James's phrase). The shift in emphasis here runs parallel to Leavis's theory of language, from viewing language as a trace of culture in his early work to its becoming one with life. The movement further from this position to his concept of an all-encompassing language is indeed a natural transition (as we have seen in chapter 3). Language now becomes truly "organic" with its capacity to maintain tradition while simultaneously continuing to change and grow. No wonder then that the writers' contribution is also assessed by Leavis in terms of their ability to adhere to this principle of tradition and continuity. Leavis's idea of a collective participation in the making of language in turn informs his study of men in relation to one another, especially in his criticism of the novel. The theoretical undergirding is an assumed commitment to the organic, community life (whether implicit as in his criticism of poetry or explicit as in his discussion of the novel). A consideration of Leavis's oeuvre makes us see the developing perception of an interdependence and interweaving of language, culture, literature and life.

# NOTES

1. F.R. Leavis, "Why Universities?" *Scrutiny* 3.2 (1934): 126.
2. Anne Samson, *F.R. Leavis* (New York: Harvester Wheatsheaf, 1992) 99.
3. Leavis, "In Defence of Milton," Rev. of *Milton and Wordsworth*, by H.J.C. Grierson and *The Miltonic Setting*, by E.M.W. Tillyard, *Scrutiny* 7.1 (1938): 113-14.
4. Leavis, *Education and the University* (1943; London: Chatto & Windus, 1972) 48-49.
5. Leavis, "English Poetry in the Seventeenth Century," *Scrutiny* 4.3 (1935): 237.
6. Leavis, "English Poetry in the Eighteenth Century," *Scrutiny* 5.1 (1936): 21-22.
7. Leavis, "Justifying One's Valuation of Blake," *The Critic as*

*Anti-Philosopher*, ed. G.S. Singh (London: Chatto & Windus, 1982) 11.

8. Leavis, "English Poetry in the Eighteenth Century," 23.
9. Leavis, "Revaluations (II): The Poetry of Pope," *Scrutiny* 2.3 (1933): 277.
10. Leavis, "English Poetry in the Seventeenth Century," 262.
11. Leavis, "Literature and Society," *Scrutiny* 12.1 (1943): 6.
12. Leavis, "English Poetry in the Eighteenth Century," 29.
13. Leavis, "'Thought' and Emotional Quality: Notes in the Analysis of Poetry," *Scrutiny* 13.1 (1945): 68.
14. Leavis, "Revaluations (IX): Keats," *Scrutiny* 4.4 (1936): 379.
15. A.C. Goodson, *Verbal Imagination* (New York: Oxford University Press, 1988) 15.
16. Goodson's displeasure with Leavis springs from Leavis's denunciation of Shelley based on what Goodson terms as Leavis's literalist conception of metaphor, which is inconsistent with his justification of Hopkins's use of metaphor; Leavis defends Hopkins on the ground that metaphor need not mean a "point-for-point" parallel. However, it is not fair to conclude that Leavis's attack on Shelley represents a growing attachment in Leavis's criticism to words as names or things. To reduce the complexity of Leavis's metaphor of organism for language to a narrow mimetic view as Goodson does (drawing support from Eagleton) is to misrepresent Leavis. Goodson's displeasure is understandable, however, considering Leavis's refusal to acknowledge the idea of organicity in Coleridge.
17. Leavis, "Revaluations (IX): Keats," 398.
18. Leavis, "Revaluations (IV): Gerard Manley Hopkins," *Scrutiny* 12.2 (1944): 84.
19. Leavis, "Revaluations (IV): Gerard Manley Hopkins," 86.
20. Leavis, "Milton's Verse," *Scrutiny*, 2.2 (1933): 129.
21. Leavis, "Milton's Verse," 129.
22. Leavis, "Milton's Verse," 130.
23. Leavis, "English Poetry in the Seventeenth Century," *Scrutiny* 4.3 (1935): 251.
24. Leavis, "English Poetry in the Seventeenth Century," 252.
25. Leavis, "English Poetry in the Seventeenth Century," 252.
26. Leavis, "'Antony and Cleopatra' and 'All for Love': A Critical Exercise," *Scrutiny* 5.2 (1936): 158.
27. Leavis, "'Antony and Cleopatra,'" 165.
28. Leavis, "'Antony and Cleopatra,'" 167.

29. Leavis, "Revaluations (VIII): Shelley," *Scrutiny* 4.2 (1935): 161-62.
30. Leavis, "Revaluations (VIII): Shelley," 160.
31. Leavis, "'Thought' and Emotional Quality," 60.
32. Leavis, "Revaluations (VIII): Shelley," 166.
33. Leavis, "Revaluations (VIII): Shelley," 178.
34. Leavis, "Revaluations (VIII): "Shelley," 180.
35. Leavis, *New Bearings in English Poetry: A Study of the Contemporary Situation* (1932; London: Chatto & Windus, 1961) 76.
36. Leavis, *New Bearings* 78.
37. Leavis, *New Bearings* 83.
38. Leavis, *The Living Principle: English as a Discipline of Thought* (London: Chatto & Windus, 1977) 156.
39. Leavis, *Living Principle* 156.
40. Leavis, *Living Principle* 171.
41. Leavis, *Living Principle* 179.
42. Leavis, *Living Principle* 191-92.
43. Leavis, *Living Principle* 226.
44. F.R. Leavis and Q.D. Leavis, *Dickens the Novelist* (1970; Harmondsworth: Penguin Books, 1980) 312.
45. F.R. Leavis and Q.D. Leavis, *Dickens* 302.
46. F.R. Leavis and Q.D. Leavis, *Dickens* 355.
47. Leavis, *Valuation in Criticism and Other Essays*, ed. G. Singh (Cambridge: Cambridge University Press, 1986) 289.
48. Merle E. Brown, "The Idea of Communal Creativity in F.R. Leavis's Recent Criticism," *Double Lyric: Divisiveness and Communal Creativity in Recent English Poetry* (London: Routledge and Kegan Paul, 1980), 212-13.
49. Leavis, *D.H. Lawrence: Novelist* (1955; Harmondsworth: Penguin Books, 1981) 122.
50. D.H. Lawrence, *Psychoanalysis and the Unconscious* as quoted by Leavis in *Thought, Words and Creativity: Art and Thought in Lawrence* (New York: Oxford University Press, 1976) 24.
51. Leavis, *Thought* 24.
52. Leavis, *The Great Tradition* (1948; Harmondsworth: Penguin Books, 1980) 16.
53. Leavis, *Great Tradition* 60.
54. Leavis, *Great Tradition* 70.
55. Leavis, *Great Tradition* 169.
56. Leavis, *Great Tradition* 189.
57. Leavis, *Anna Karenina and Other Essays* quoted from R.P. Bilan, *The Literary Criticism of F.R. Leavis* (Cambridge: Cambridge

University Press, 1979) 110-11.

58. Francis Mulhern, "English Reading" in *Nation and Narration*, ed. Homi K. Bhabha (London: Routledge, 1990) 254-55.
59. Leavis, *Great Tradition* 224.
60. If we extend Benedict Anderson's idea of imagined communities, [Benedict Anderson, *Imagined Communities: Reflections on the Origin and Spread of Nationalism* (1983; London: Verso, 1992)] is it possible for us to see Leavis's construction of the English nation (not limited to the geographical space) as an imagined community of all those who share a common language and literature and a world obtainable through them? Would it then signal the emergence of a new English nation severed from the Latin parent? Viewed thus, Leavis can be regarded as an inheritor of a tradition of anti-Latin and pro-English education starting from Matthew Arnold. When the departure from education in Latin is made towards English studies, the "sharedness" of community-relations, which makes them constitute a new nation, can no longer be inherited, but consciously acquired. Hence, Leavis's insistence that the old "organic" community values cannot be historically obtained, but only recreated in and through a study of literature and practice of literary criticism.
61. Leavis, *Great Tradition* 262-63.
62. F.R. Leavis and Q.D. Leavis, *Dickens* 286.
63. F.R. Leavis and Q.D. Leavis, *Dickens* 304-05.
64. F.R. Leavis and Q.D. Leavis, *Dickens* 334.
65. F.R. Leavis and Q.D. Leavis, *Dickens* 359.
66. Leavis, *D.H. Lawrence* 120.
67. Leavis, *D.H. Lawrence* 120.
68. Leavis, *D.H.Lawrence* 122.
69. Leavis, *Thought* 22.
70. Leavis, *Thought* 26.
71. Leavis, "Joyce and 'The Revolution of the Word,'" *Scrutiny* 2.2 (1933): 196.
72. Leavis, "E.M. Forster," *Scrutiny* 7.2 (1939): 188.
73. Leavis, "E.M. Forster," 200.
74. Leavis, "After 'To the Lighthouse,'" *Scrutiny* 10.3 (1942): 296-97.
75. Leavis, "After 'To the Lighthouse,'" 298.
76. Leavis, "The Irony of Swift," *Scrutiny* 2.4 (1934): 377.
77. Leavis, "The Irony of Swift," 377.
78. Leavis, "The Irony of Swift," 378.
79. R.P. Bilan, *The Literary Criticism of F.R. Leavis* (Cambridge: Cambridge University Press, 1979) 105.

80. David Lodge, *Language of Fiction*, quoted in R.P. Bilan, *The Literary Criticism of F.R. Leavis* 108.
81. Leavis, *The Great Tradition*, quoted in R.P. Bilan, The Literary Criticism of F.R. Leavis 113.
82. Terry Eagleton, *Literary Theory* (Oxford: Basil and Blackwell, 1983) 51.
83. John Gross, in an interview with Philip French in "Dr Leavis and the Drift of Civilization," *Three Honest Men: A Critical Mosaic*, by Philip French (Manchester: Carcanet New Press, 1980) 62.

# Chapter 5

## "In-conclusion"

> The critic, one would suppose, if he is to justify his existence, should endeavour to discipline his personal prejudices and cranks—traces to which we are all subject—and compose his differences with as many of his fellows as possible, in the common pursuit of true judgment.
>
> (T.S. Eliot, "The Function of Criticism," 1923, rpt. in *Selected Essays* [1932], 1976, 25)

> Out of agreement and disagreement with particular judgments of value a sense of relative value in the concrete will define itself, and, without this, no amount of talk about 'values' in the abstract is worth anything.
>
> (F.R. Leavis, "Restatement for Critics," *Scrutiny*, 1.4, 1933, 319)

The consideration we have made in the foregoing chapters is that of Leavis's views on language, literature, community and culture, his felt need to reconstitute the values of the historically lost organic community to fight forces of disintegration in the "technologico-Benthamite" civilization of the modern world, the possibility of reconstruction of a civilized community in its place through literature and literary criticism in the University, the importance of the training of intelligence and sensibility through a study of one's own language (and hence the questions of English and Englishness) and how far all these ideas inform Leavis's critical practice. Despite its pervading presence in various ramifications, the question of the organic community and ideas related to it have received insufficient attention in the large corpus of criticism on Leavis. Critics who have addressed this question have invariably talked about its historical aspect and viewed it as a romantic escape into an unobtainable past. An attempt has been made in the preceding chapters to demonstrate how the concept becomes a living presence in Leavis's critical theory and practice.

This chapter attempts to examine the more or less incidental ideas of various critics bearing on the theme of organic community and to see them in relation to the questions raised so far. It hopes to arrive at some tentative judgements on these issues in the spirit of a collaborative critical pursuit, a spirit Leavis had endeavoured to promote.

The question of the individual and society comes up very often in an evaluation of Leavis's criticism. Marc De la Ruelle in his "The Ideological Roots of Cultural Studies in England" traces the beginnings of the movement of cultural studies to the liberal humanist tradition starting from Matthew Arnold. He, however, sees a difference, and rightly so, in the relative emphasis the present movement of cultural studies and the liberal humanist tradition lay on the individual and society. He points out that

> [f]or Williams, it was basically social, representing the collective idea, while so-called bourgeois culture stressed individual, intellectual and imaginative work. In political terms, this was the opposition between socialism and liberalism, although Williams did not use these terms.[1]

This emphasis on the difference between the "socialist" and liberal-humanist ways is necessary because their discourse seems at times to be almost indistinguishable. This reminds us of our discussion of the collaborative nature of Volosinov's and Leavis's critical theory. Ruelle's identification of the difference between the "socialist" and the liberal-humanist emphasis on the individual and society helps us to reiterate the point that Leavis and Volosinov (as with Leavis and Williams here) depart from each other on the question of the primacy they give to the individual and society.

How does Leavis's emphasis on the individual stand in relation to his programme of Education? In their study of "Academic English and the Common Reader," Kaplan and Rose point to a contradiction in New Criticism and Leavis between the use of close reading as a pedagogical tool, a specialized activity capable of being practised by a limited few and the "populist" or "democratic" impulse.[2] We may recall here our discussion in chapter 3 regarding David Holbrook's remark that Leavis's enthusiasm for training an elite gets the better of his commitment to philosophical or essential questions. The logical outcome of a stress on the democratic impulse ought to have helped Leavis to engage in a true dialogue with his adversaries in the spirit of the mutual collaboration he had himself propagated. In a reading of the *Scrutiny* movement which ironically goes a little overboard because of its inattention to the contribution of the Leavises, Iain Wright demonstrates, among other things, how a real possibility of a common programme with the Left is thwarted by Leavis's refusal to critically communicate with his opponents.[3]

If a genuine dialogue was indeed absent in Leavis's engagement with his critics, how do we re-view his concept of the organic community? Lesley Johnson is quite perceptive in relating the issue of the training of the elite to the concept of the organic community in Leavis. He says:

> The idea of the organic community in Leavis's work needs to be examined in relationship to his argument for a system of elites. The idea of a past form of society in which everyone had an accepted function dictated by a 'natural order' establishes a mythical version of the desirable (but lost) form of society. The only way to restore some semblance of this society, he could then go on to say, is through a system of elites or oligarchic structures, on the basis of which the social function of at least certain groups will be restored. The organic society couched in terms of a golden age legitimates this hierarchical vision of society in which the literary intellectuals have a specific and powerful function to fulfil.[4]

Leavis's problem, as diagnosed by Johnson, was to reconcile democracy with the maintenance of high standards. Johnson refers to Leavis's statement that if democracy was equated with the lowering of standards he would not mind opposing it. He also offers his opinion on the idea of collaboration in Leavis. While he feels that a collaborative exchange of judgement failed to take place in Leavis's own engagement with other writers, *Scrutiny* could have provided it:

> *Scrutiny* provided a place in which that collaborative exchange, which Leavis held to be so important to literary criticism, could be carried out (within certain limits). It also provided a means by which the ideas of Leavis and others on educational and social issues could be disseminated. The fact that it was a journal which catered explicitly for a minority led inevitably to its failure. It could only disseminate its ideas amongst those already converted.[5]

Yes, genuine exchange seems to have been possible only among people who have already accepted a set of values. Colin Evans in his *English People* refers to Walsh's comments on the "Leavisite" consensus: "The canon could change (unlike in classics) but the criteria for inclusion were fixed. They had to do with complexity and seriousness as against gentility."[6] It is interesting to see how Evans is able to turn even the adulatory Walsh to his own advantage. He goes on to say that "[t]he belief was that studying English would make people more moral and would enable them to lead better lives amid the pressures of the modern world. English was *redemptive.*"[7]

Raymond Williams in his *Culture and Society* exposes the narrowness of Leavis's understanding of the role of English. He says that English can be redemptive only if it is able to encompass the whole culture. He goes on: "For experience that is formally recorded we go, not only to the rich source of literature, but also to history, building, painting, music, philosophy, theology, political and social theory, the physical and natural sciences, anthropology, and indeed the whole body of learning."[8] As against this ever-widening scope of culture, Leavis concentrates on the minority culture and its promotion through the study of English and criticism. Williams argues that Leavis's "concept of a cultivated minority, set over against a 'decreated' mass, tends in its assertion, to a damaging arrogance and scepticism. The concept of a wholly organic and satisfying past, to be set over against a disintegrated and dissatisfying present, tends in its neglect of history to a denial of real and social experience."[9] He considers it ". . . foolish and dangerous to exclude from the so called organic society the penury, the petty tyranny, the disease and mortality, the ignorance and frustrated intelligence which were also among its ingredients."[10]

That brings us to the question of the historicity of the organic community as a recurrent one in a study of Leavis. The homogeneousness and organicity of the seventeenth and early eighteenth century culture as postulated by Leavis do come in for some severe criticism based on the fact that these societies represented a clear demarcation of people on economic terms. Leavis's statement that a Shakespeare play appealed at different "levels" of response itself could testify to the existence of a heterogeneous society. If so, how do we interpret Leavis's continuous harping on the question of organic community? Leavis's emphasis is not so much on whether the seventeenth and early eighteenth centuries were organic communities, as on whether it was not possible for writers at that time to produce works which appealed simultaneously to the sophisticated and the popular because they both shared one and the same language. The ungrudging acceptance of those in the lower rungs of the unequal system might have given a semblance of homogeneity to these societies. What appeals to Leavis is not so much the idea of homogeneity, but the idea of the organism, with its interrelated parts, which to him stands for individuals' assigned role in the total community. This explains Leavis's emphasis on men in relation to one another in his study of the novel, though in reality he was not thinking of the whole society as is evident from his statements against mass literacy.

In this context, Eugene Goodheart's essay on the organic society in Leavis too raises some interesting questions. He says that what Leavis says about the living speech in the work of Shakespeare and Donne is also true of Jane Austen, George Eliot and D.H. Lawrence. He goes on to observe that "[t]he living speech of great poets and novelists is the revelation of the inter-connectedness of people within a living community or what Burke, Coleridge, Carlyle indeed, virtually every significant writer since the eighteenth century understood as the organic society."[11] Goodheart's agreeing with what Leavis is said to have implied about the work of the writers since the eighteenth century is somewhat intriguing on two counts. Leavis does not imply that the living speech of the great poets and novelists since the eighteenth century reveals the inter-connectedness of people within the communities which the writers represent, for Leavis is aware and has declared openly that organic communities are no longer found after 1700. His statement could only mean that the communities the writers represent in their work (which may be different from their own) reveal the inter-connectedness of people, which is reflected in the living speech of the characters. Leavis's programme to reconstruct the values of the organic community involves a constant restatement of those values to provide a chief incitement towards the new. Goodheart's statement is also surprising because he realizes the difference between an unrecoverable past and a living present. This ought to have led him to understand that what Leavis is talking about is simultaneously an unrecoverable past (in the form of loss of organic community historically) and an assertion of its living presence in the form of the best literature. It is his inability to understand this distinction that makes him find Leavis's view of the organic society ambiguous. He says: "On the one hand, he [Leavis] suggests that what is real for literature may be an unrealized ideal for society. On the other hand, the organic society is conceived as an ideal for literature itself, which in Leavis's view is threatened by the same corruption one discovers in society."[12] It is an unrealized ideal for society because Leavis is sure that we cannot historically recover the organic society. It is a recoverable ideal for literature (as has been achieved in the works of his "great" writers), though literature too continues to be threatened by corruptive forces of advertising, journalism, film etc. The strength of Goodheart's essay, however, lies in pointing out Leavis's unwillingness to accept any negation of the life principle in writers like Eliot, Joyce and Beckett, even though such negation is more realistic than the romantic pictures of life Leavis appreciates in the writers of his great tradition. Goodheart is also able to pinpoint Leavis's strengths as well as weaknesses, as in the following statements:

> Leavis's conception of literature as a community with the attributes of organic life implies a symbiosis between art and

> life that modern literary theory and practical criticism often deny in an exclusive attention to the internal history of literature.
>
> . . . Leavis's failure as a critic on his own terms is his unwillingness or inability to engage the adversary or the other (whoever or whatever it may be) in a dialectical—or should I say communal—exchange.[13]

The issue of the organic society Goodheart takes up raises nevertheless some important questions. If we agree that works of art are produced under certain historical conditions, and that they are also studied and interpreted under possibly different historical conditions, we have to accept the notion of inevitable change. If so, we wonder how Leavis expects the writers after the loss of organic community to reproduce (i.e., maintain) the values of the organic community. How does the maintenance of the values reconcile itself with the principle of inevitable change? In fact, Leavis's emphasis on the metaphor of the organism and his insistence on the living principle implying growth and change conflict with his assertion of the continuance of certain values of the organic community. Even if some writers consciously strive to revive the values, is it possible for the readers who are not just the writers' own contemporaries to accept them, situated as they may be under different historical conditions? Leavis's grand design is possible of achievement only if great writers he has in mind and the readership which reads them share certain common interests. What Leavis is looking forward to is a reconstruction of a homogeneous community that includes the writers, the literary critics and a broad readership. His programme of education through the English School at the university is geared towards the establishment of this cultivated minority.

Glenn Most cautions us against harping on the question of this seemingly obvious contradiction in Leavis's organicist model. What he values most in Leavis is the supreme principle of life that characterizes literature itself—". . . a principle of continuity and creativity, most obviously present in natural language, which transcends and grounds the individuality of the artist, who by subordinating himself to it alone can truly realize himself."[14] We can agree with Most that language does have this unique capacity to maintain a level of continuity while it simultaneously changes The significance of the metaphor of the organism for language and literature begins to make more sense now. The language also implies a collective effort even as individual speakers keep adapting it to their own tastes and contributing to it. Most also sees the value of "life" in Leavis in relation to the dichotomy he draws from Blake between "selfhood" and "identity." (We have discussed the importance of these terms in chapter 3.) This also reminds us of Anne Samson's statement regarding the development in Leavis's thought from his considering language as a reflection of culture in his early days to his being convinced by the end of his career, of culture being but a trace of language. Michael Bell's study in which he tries to see the affinity of Leavis's conception of language with that of Heidegger is useful here. He says: "Language is the historical creation of its community and conditions prereflectively the nature of its particular world."[15] He also says that this historical nature of language lends the impersonal dimension to even the personal act of speech. Language in this sense, for Leavis, encompasses history. It is the inability of some critics to understand this conception of language that makes them see Leavis as being inattentive to history.[16] Bell is right in pointing out the lacuna in Raymond Williams's reading of Leavis's organic community, which also results from a similar lack of understanding:

> When Williams suggests that Leavis should include more cultural elements than the literary in his analysis, he is selling Leavis's position short. He exemplifies once again the persistent misunderstanding of what the 'literary' would encompass for Leavis. Leavis's proposed study of the seventeenth century, for example, would have encompassed all fields of enquiry and achievement. The difference is that he would have considered them as forms of language.[17]

The strength of Bell's and Most's study lies in their recognition of the resemblance between Leavis's invitation to readers to participate in the text's unfolding itself and the hermeneutic circle. The part-whole analogy they allude to and its relationship to Leavis's organicist model cannot be missed. Leavis's movement towards a language which subsumes culture also seems close to the poststructuralist emphasis on the self-referentiality of language. But, for Leavis, as has been made clear in our discussion of him in relation to Bloom and Miller, language is not self-referential. It is just that language includes culture in all its manifestations. For the Marxist, on the other hand, language is perhaps but one form of culture. However, when the very Marxism (which Leavis has opposed throughout his career) is reviewing the role of superstructural elements (even as it continues to emphasize the ultimate economic determinants), Leavis's own conception of language and his attempts to recover the values of the organic community through its traces in a still existing positive tradition in literature may have to be taken more seriously.

A word in the end about the nature of Leavis's criticism. To the extent he questions the whole Western tradition starting from Descartes, he anticipates the deconstructionists in that both Leavis and the deconstructionists question the rational basis of the self's understanding of the world. While for Leavis the understanding takes place in the continuous collaborative exchanges between the self and the other, for the deconstructionists it is intersubjective giving rise to endless deferral of meaning. Nevertheless, Leavis is a very staunch liberal humanist, who argues for a stable order, the order of the like in the organic communities. To the extent he disturbs the authority of the author and shifts the emphasis to a community of critics and readers, he is a precursor to the reader response critics. But in cultivating a privileged, power group of the elite through his critical endeavour he is criti-thoritative (if we may coin a term to describe him) in his ability to manufacture a consensus. To the extent he emphasizes the socio-cultural-historical contexts in his criticism, he is a Marxist or cultural theorist. But to the extent he denounces the economic base of society, he is anti-Marxist. To the extent he makes explicit use of the philosophers he is a theorist. To the extent he relies heavily on the words on the page and refuses to make theoretical formulations, he is a professed anti-philosopher. To the extent he opposes every establishment he is anti-authority. To the extent he nurtures and rears a whole critical establishment he wields authority and controls literary taste. To critically "place" this complex and conflicting nature of

Leavis's contribution has been and continues to be a stupendous task.

# NOTES

1. Marc De la Ruelle, "The Ideological Roots of Cultural Studies in England," *English Studies in Transition: Papers from the ESSE Inaugural Conference*, eds. Robert Clark and Piero Boitani (London: Routledge, 1993) 102.
2. Carey Kaplan and Ellen Cronan Rose, "Academic English and the Common Reader," *The Canon and the Common Reader* (Knoxville: The University of Tennessee Press, 1990) 52.
3. Iain Wright, "F.R. Leavis, the *Scrutiny* Movement and the Crisis," *Culture and Crisis in Britain in the Thirties* (London: Lawrence and Wishart, 1979) 37-65.
4. Lesley Johnson, *The Cultural Critics: From Matthew Arnold to Raymond Williams* (London: Routledge & Kegan Paul, 1979) 97.
5. Lesley Johnson, 115.
6. Colin Evans, *English People: The Experience of Teaching and Learning English in British Universities* (Buckingham: Open University Press, 1993) 131.
7. Colin Evans, 131.
8. Raymond Williams, *Culture and Society: 1780-1950* (1958; London: Chatto & Windus, 1967) 248.
9. Raymond Williams 256.
10. Raymond Williams 253.
11. Eugene Goodheart, "The Organic Society of F.R. Leavis," *The Failure of Criticism* (Cambridge: Harvard University Press, 1978) 70.
12. Eugene Goodheart, "The Organic Society," 75.
13. Eugene Goodheart, "The Organic Society," 82-83.
14. Glenn Most, "Principled Reading," *Diacritics*, June 1979: 60.
15. Michael Bell, *F.R. Leavis* (London: Routledge, 1988) 43.
16. I have tried to argue out a case for the historical nature of Leavis's criticism in my response to Hiren Gohain in "Leavis's Romantic Connection: A Response," *Journal of Contemporary Thought* (1991): 97-98.
17. Michael Bell, *F.R. Leavis* 117.

# Select Bibliography

## Articles


Aithal, S. Krishnamoorthy. "Leavis as an Analytical Critic." *The Literary Criterion* 12.4 (1977): 71-84.

______. "The Use of Interpretation in the Criticism of F.R. Leavis." *British Journal of Aesthetics* 18.4 (1978): 342-44.

Anderson, Perry. "Components of the National Culture." *English Questions*. London: Verso, 1992. 96-103.

Bantock, G.H. "Some Cultural Implications of Freedom in Education." *Scrutiny* 15.2 (1948): 82-97.

Bateson, F.W. and F.R.Leavis. "Correspondence: The Responsible Critic." *Scrutiny* 19.4 (1953): 317-28.

Bergonzi, Bernard. "Leavis and Eliot: The Long Road to Rejection." *Critical Quarterly* 26.1 & 2 (1984): 21-43.

Betsky, Seymour et al. "F.R. Leavis: Stability and Growth." *The New Universities Quarterly* 30.1 (1975): 66-106.

Black, Michael. "The Language, Culture and the Community." *The Use of English* 21.1 (1969): 42-46.

______. "Leavis, Lawrence: Extending Limits." Rev. of *Thought, Words and Creativity*, by F.R. Leavis. *English* 26.124 (1977): 23-40.

______. "The Third Realm." *The Use of English* 15 (1964):280-88.

______. "The Third Realm: Part II." *The Use of English* 16.1 (1964): 21-31.

Bredin, Hugh. "F.R. Leavis's Theory of Language in *The Living Principle*." *Critical Quarterly* 24.2 (1982): 61-68.

Buckley, Vincent. "Leavis and His 'Line.'" *The Critical Review* 8 (1965): 110-20.

Byrne, Peter. "Leavis, Literary Criticism and Philosophy." *British Journal of Aesthetics* 19.3 (1979): 263-73.

Carey, Hugh. "The English School." *Mansfield Forbes and His Cambridge*. Cambridge: Cambridge University Press, 1984. 62-74.

Cordner, Christopher. "F.R.Leavis and the Moral in Literature." *On Literary Theory and Philosophy*. Eds. Richard Fredman and Lloyd Reinhardt. New York: St. Martin's Press, 1991. 60-81.

Coyne, Pat. "Two Cultures Revisited." *New Statesman and Society*. Oct. 1993: 30-31.

Doyle, Brian. "Invention of English." *Englishness: Politics and Culture 1880-1920*. Eds. Robert Colls and Philip Dodd. London: Croomhelm,

1986. 89-115.

Eliot, T.S. "Yeats." *Selected Prose of T.S. Eliot*. Ed. Frank Kermode. London: Faber and Faber, 1975. 248-57.

Farley-Hills, D.L. "Dr. Leavis's Critical Apologia." *Criticism* 2.2 (1961): 95-100.

Felperin, Howard. "Leavisism Revisited." *Beyond Deconstruction: The Uses and Absues of Literary Theory*. Oxford: Clarendon Press, 1985. 6-49.

Fish, Stanley. "Is There a Text in This Class?" *Contemporary Criticism: An Anthology*. Ed. V.S. Seturaman. Madras: Macmillan, 1989. 276-92.

Fergusson, Francis. "On F.R.Leavis." *Literary Landmarks: Essays on the Theory and Practice of Literature*. New Brunswick: Rutgers University Press, 1975. 131-36.

Fraser, John. "Reflections on Organic Community." *The Human World* 15 & 16 (1974): 57-74.

Goode, John. "The Moment of *Scrutiny*." New Left Review 122 (1980): 90-96.

Goodheart, Eugene. "The Organic Society of F.R.Leavis." *The Failure of Criticism*. Cambridge: Harvard University Press, 1978. 68-83.

Gribble, James. "Logical and Psychological Considerations in the Criticism of F.R. Leavis." *British Journal of Aesthetics* 10.1 (1970): 39-57.

Harding, D.W. "T.S.Eliot, 1925-1935." Rev. of *Collected Poems 1909-1935* by T.S. Eliot. *Scrutiny* 2 (1936): 171-76.

______. "We Have Not Reached Conclusion." Rev. of *Little Gidding* by T.S. Eliot. *Scrutiny* 11.3 (1943): 216-19.

Harvey, John. "F.R. Leavis." *Encounter* 52.5 (1979): 59-67.

Heyl, Bernard. "The Absolutism of F.R.Leavis." *The Journal of Aesthetics and Art Criticism* 13.2 (1954): 249-55.

Iyer, Ramaswamy R. "Leavis on *Four Quartets*: A Critique of Leavis's *The Living Principle*." *The Literary Criterion* 27.4 (1992): 42-52.

Jarrett-Kerr, Martin. "The Literary Criticism of Leavis." *Essays in Criticism* 2.4 (1952): 351-68.

Kaplan, Carey and Ellen Cronan Rose. "Academic English and the Common Reader." *The Canon and the Common Reader*. Knoxville: The University of Tennessee Press, 1990. 47-65.

Karlekar, Ranajay. "F.R.Leavis: Specialist of Wholeness." *Essays and Studies* 6 (1987): 179-92.

Killham, John. "The Use of 'Concreteness' as an Evaluative Term in F.R.Leavis's *The Great Tradition*." *The British Journal of Aesthetics* 5.1 (1965): 14-24.

Klingopulos, G.D. "English Literature and the University." *The Use of English* 22.1 (1970): 14-20.

Knights, L.C. "Remembering *Scrutiny*." *The Sewanee Review* LXXXIX. 4 (1981): 560-85.

Leavis, F.R. "Advanced Verbal Education." Rev. of *The Philosophy of Rhetoric*, by I.A. Richards and *Scepticism and Poetry*, by D.G. James. *Scrutiny* 6.2 (1937): 211-17.

______. "After Ten Years." *Scrutiny* 10.4 (1942): 326-28.

______. "After 'To the Lighthouse.'" *Scrutiny* 7.2 (1942): 296-97.

______. "'Antony and Cleopatra' and 'All for Love': A Critical Excercise." *Scrutiny* 5.2 (1936): 158-69.

______. "Appreciation of Henry James." *Scrutiny* 14.3 (1947): 229-37.

______. "Approaches to T.S. Eliot." *Scrutiny* 15.1 (1947): 56-67.

______. "Arnold's Thought." *Scrutiny* 8.1 (1939): 92-99.

______. "Auden, Bottrall and Others." *Scrutiny* 3.1 (1934): 70-83.

______. "Believing in University." *The Human World* 15 & 16 (1974): 98-110.

______. "Comments and Reviews: 'Little Gidding.'" *Scrutiny* 12.1 (1943): 58.

______. "Correspondence: Lawrence and Eliot." *Scrutiny* 18.2 (1951): 136-43.

______. "Criticism of Shakespeare's Late Plays." *Scrutiny* 10.4 (1942): 339-45.

______. "Dostoevsky or Dickens." *Scrutiny* 2.1 (1933): 91-93.

______. "D.H. Lawrence and Professor Irving Babbit." Rev. of *The Letters of D.H.Lawrence*, ed. with an Introduction by Aldous Huxley. *Scrutiny* 1.3 (1932): 273-79.

______. "The Dunciad." Rev. of *The Poems of Alexander Pope. Scrutiny* 12.1 (1943): 74-80.

______. "Mr. Eliot and Education." Rev. of *Essays Ancient and Modern* by T.S. Eliot. *Scrutiny* 5.1 (1936): 84-89.

______. "Mr Eliot and Lawrence." Revs. of *D.H. Lawrence and Human Existence*, by Father William Tiverton with Foreword by T.S.Eliot and *Portion of a Genius, But...*, by Richard Aldington. *Scrutiny* 18.1 (1951): 66-73.

______. "Eliot's Later Poetry." Rev. of *The Dry Salvages* by T.S. Eliot. *Scrutiny* 11.1 (1942): 60-71.

______. "E.M. Forster." *Scrutiny* 7.2 (1939): 185-202.

______. "English Poetry in the Seventeenth Century." *Scrutiny* 4.3 (1935): 236-56.

______. "English Poetry in the Eighteenth Century." *Scrutiny* 5.1 (1936): 13-31.

______. "Fate of Edward Thomas." *Scrutiny* 7.4 (1939): 441-43.

______. "Imagery and Movement: Notes in the Analysis of Poetry." *Scrutiny* 13.2 (1945): 119-34.

______. "In Defence of Milton." Revs. of *Milton and Wordworth* by Sir H.J.C. Grierson and *The Miltonic Setting* by E.M.W. Tillyard. *Scrutiny* 7.1 (1938): 104-14.

______. "Introduction." in Marius Bewley. *The Complex Fate: Hawthorne, Henry James and Some Other American Writers*. New York: Gordian Press, 1967. vii-xv.
______. "The Irony of Swift." *Scrutiny* 2.4 (1934): 364-78.
______. "Johnson." *Scrutiny* 11.1 (1942): 75-78.
______. "Joyce and 'The Revolution of the Word.'" *Scrutiny* 2.2 (1933): 193-201.
______. "Latest Yeats." *Scrutiny* 2.3 (1933): 293-95.
______. "The Letters of Gerard Manley Hopkins." *Scrutiny* 4.2 (1935): 216-31.
______. "Literature and Society." *Scrutiny* 12.1 (1943): 2-11.
______. "Literary Criticism and Philosophy: A Reply." *Scrutiny* 6.1 (1937): 59-70.
______. "The Literary Mind." *Scrutiny* 1.1 (1932): 20-32.
______. "'Little Gidding.'" *Scrutiny* 12.1 (1943): 58.
______. "Mass Civilization and Minority Culture." In Appendix III of *Education and the University: A Sketch for an English School*. London: Chatto & Windus, 1943. 141-71.
______. "Milton's Verse." *Scrutiny* 2.2 (1933): 123-36.
______. "More Lawrence." *Scrutiny* 1.4 (1933): 404-05.
______. "Objections to a Review of 'Little Gidding.'" *Scrutiny* 9.3 (1940): 259-67.
______. "Poet as Executant." Rev. of *Four Quartets* by T.S. Eliot. *Scrutiny* 15.1 (1947): 68-80.
______. "Pope on the Upswing." *Scrutiny* 8.2 (1939): 237-40.
______. "'The Portrait of a Lady' Reprinted." *Scrutiny* 15.3 (1948): 235-41.
______. "Reminiscences of D.H. Lawrence." *Scrutiny* 1.2 (1932): 189-91.
______. "Restatement for Critics." *Scrutiny* 1.4 (1933): 315-23.
______. "Revaluations (II): The Poetry of Pope." *Scrutiny* 2.3 (1933): 268-84.
______. "Revaluations (IV): Gerard Manley Hopkins." *Scrutiny* 12.2 (1944): 82-93.
______. "Revaluations (VIII): Shelley." *Scrutiny* 6.2 (1933): 158-80.
______. "Revaluations (IX): Keats." *Scrutiny* 4.4 (1936): 376-400.
______. "This Poetical Renascence." *Scrutiny* 2.1 (1933): 65-76.
______. "Thought and Emotional Quality." *Scrutiny* 13.1 (1945): 53-71.
______. "What's Wrong with Criticism." *Scrutiny* 1.2 (1932): 132-46.
______. "Why Universities?" *Scrutiny* 3.2 (1934): 117-32.
______. "The Wild, Untutored Phoenix." *Scrutiny* 6.3 (1937): 352-58.
Lucas, John. "Yes, But Hang on a Minute." *Moderns & Contemporaries: Novelists, Poets, Critics*. Sussex: The Harvester Press, 1985. 151-59.
MacCabe, Colin. "Towards a Modern Trivium: English Studies Today." *Critical Quarterly* 26.1 & 2 (1984): 69-82.

McLuhan, H.M. "Poetic vs Rhetorical Exegesis: The Case for Leavis against Richards and Empson." *The Sewanee Review* 52 (1944): 267-76.

Martin, W.R. "Casterbridge and the Organic Community." *The Use of English* 12.1 (1960): 30-33.

Mason, H.A. "Wounded Surgeons." *The Cambridge Quarterly* 11.1 (1982): 189-222.

Miller, J. Hillis. "Tradition and Difference." Rev. of *Natural Supernaturalism: Tradition and Revolution* in *Romantic Literature* by M.H. Abrams. *Diacritics* Winter (1972): 6-11.

Morton, A.L. "Culture and Leisure." *Scrutiny* 1.4 (1933): 324-26.

Most, Glenn W. "Principled Reading." *Diacritics* June 1979: 53-64.

Mulhern, Francis. "English Reading." *Nation and Narration.* Ed. Homi Bhabha. London: Routledge, 1990. 250-64.

Newton, J.M. "At the Mill with Slaves." Rev. of *Thought, Words and Creativity* by F.R. Leavis. *The Cambridge Quarterly* 7.3 (1977): 245-51.

Pradhan, S.V. "Literary Criticism and Cultural Diagnosis: F.R. Leavis on W.H. Auden." *The British Journal of Aesthetics* 12.4 (1972): 384-94.

Pugh, Bridget. "The Sense of Community in George Eliot and D.H. Lawrence." *Yearly Review* 1 Dec. 1987: 66-76.

Pyle, Forest. "A Novel Sympathy: The Imagination of Community in George Eliot." *Novel* Fall 1993: 5-23.

Ringrose, C.X. "F.R. Leavis and Yvor Winters on G.M.Hopkins." *English Studies* 55.1 (1974): 32-42.

Robinson, Ian. "The Third Realm: Ten Years Work by F.R.Leavis." *The Human World* 3 (1971): 71-85.

Ruelle, Mark De la. "Ideological Roots of Cultural Studies in England." *English Studies in Transition: Papers from ESSE Inaugural Conference*. London: Routledge, 1993. 97-104.

Sreenivasan, S. "Leavis on Impersonality: The Evolution of a Critical Concept." *Journal of Literature and Aesthetics* 1.2 (1981): 77-84.

Sridhar, M. "Leavis's Romantic Connection: A Response." *Journal of Contemporary Thought* (1991): 97-106.

Strickland, Geoffrey. "The Criticism of F.R. Leavis." *Structuralism or Criticism: Thoughts on How We Read.* Cambridge: Cambridge University Press, 1981. 141-75.

______. "Great Traditions: The Logic of the Canon." *Encyclopedia of Literature and Criticism*. Eds. Martin Coyle, et al. London: Routledge, 1990. 696-707.

______. "Leavis and Lawrence: 'The Distempered Part': A Reply to H.A. Mason's 'The Wounded Surgeons.'" *The Cambridge Quarterly* 11.2 (1982): 331-38.

Taneja, G.R. "F.R. Leavis on the Function of Criticism." *Yearly Review* 7

Dec. 1993: 89-98.

Vivas, Elisio. "Mr. Leavis and D.H. Lawrence." Rev. of *D.H. Lawrence: Novelist* by F.R. Leavis. *Sewanee Review* 65 (1957): 123-36.

Walatara, Douglas. "F.R. Leavis: Educationist: A Sri Lanka View." *The Literary Criterion* 14.2 (1979): 52-70.

Walsh, J.H. "George Sturt." *The Use of English* 19.3 (1968): 195-98.

Wellek, Rene. "F.R. Leavis (1895-1978) and the *Scrutiny* Group." A History of Modern Criticism. Vol. 5. New Haven: Yale University Press. 239-64.

______. "Literary Criticism and Philosophy." *Scrutiny* 5.4 (1937): 375-83.

Wilde, Oscar. "The Critic as Artist." *The Works of Oscar Wilde*. New York: P.F. Collier & Son Corporation, 1927. 545-97.

Williams, Raymond. "Cambridge English, Past and Present." *Writing in Society*. London: Verso, 1991. 177-91.

______. "Symposium." *The Critical Quarterly* 1.3 (1958): 245-47.

Worman, Jeremy. "Texts and Traditions." Rev. of *Literary Englands: Versions of 'Englishness' in English Writing* by David Gervais. *English* 43.177 (1994): 274-76.

Wright, Iain. "F.R. Leavis, the *Scrutiny* Movement and the Crisis." Culture and Crisis in Britain in the Thirties. London: Lawrence and Wishart, 1979. 37-65.

## Books

Aithal, S.K. *F.R. Leavis on the Function of Criticism*. Ph.D. Diss. Indiana University, 1972.

Allen, Peter. *The Cambridge Apostles: The Early Years*. Cambridge: Cambridge University Press, 1978.

Anderson, Benedict. *Imagined Communities: Reflections on the Origin and Spread of Naturalism*. 1983. London: Verso, 1992.

Arnold, Matthew. *Culture and Anarchy: An Essay in Political and Social Criticism*. 1869. London: John Murray, 1956.

______. *Essays in Criticism*, 1969. Ed. S.R. Littlewood. 1938. New York: St. Martin's Press, 1966.

Baldick, Chris. *Social Mission of English Criticism 1848-1932*. Oxford: Clarendon Press, 1983.

Batsleer, Janet, Tony Davies, Rebecca O'Rourke, and Chris Weedon. *Rewriting English: Cultural Politics of Gender and Class*. London: Methuen, 1985.

Bell, Michael. *F.R. Leavis*. London: Routledge, 1988.

Belsey, Catherine. *Critical Practice*. London: Methuen, 1980.

Bentley, Eric. *The Importance of Scrutiny: A Quarterley Review, 1932-48*. 1948. New York: New York University Press, 1964.

Bergonzi, Bernard. *Exploding English: Criticism, Theory and Culture*. Oxford: Clarendon Press, 1990.

______. *Reading the Thirties*. London: Methuen, 1978.

Bilan, R.P. *The Literary Criticism of F.R. Leavis*. Cambridge: Cambridge University Press, 1979.

Bloom, Harold. *Agon: Towards a Theory of Revisionism*. New York: Oxford University Press, 1982.

Borklund, Elmer. *Contemporary Literary Critics*. Michigan: Gale Research Company, 1982.

Boyers, Robert. *F.R. Leavis: Judgment and the Discipline of Thought*. Columbia: University of Missouri Press, 1978.

Brown, Merle E. *Double Lyric: Divisiveness and Communal Creativity in Recent English Poetry*. London: Routledge and Kegan Paul, 1980.

Buckley, Vincent. *Poetry and Morality: Studies on the Criticism of Matthew Arnold, T.S.Eliot and F.R. Leavis*. 1959. London: Chatto & Windus, 1968.

Burke, Edmund. *The Writings and Speeches of Edmund Burke* Vol. 3. Boston: Little Brown Co., 1901.

Cayne, Bernard S., ed. *Encyclopedia of Americana*. 1829. New York: Americana Corporation, 1976.

Clark, Jon, et al., eds. *Culture and Crisis in Britain: The Thirties*. London: Lawrence and Wishart, 1979.

Clark, Robert and Piero Boitani, eds. *English Studies in Transition: Papers from ESSE Inaugural Conference*. London: Routledge, 1993.

Cole, G.D.H. *Social Theory*. London: Methuen & Co. Ltd., 1920.

Colls, Robert, and Philip Dodd. *Englishness: Politics and Culture 1880-1920*. London: Croom Helm, 1986.

Colmer, John. *Coleridge: Critic of Society*. Oxford: Clarendon Press, 1959.

______. *Coleridge to Catch 22: Images of Society*. London: Macmillan, 1978.

Coyle, Martin, et al. eds. *Encyclopedia of Literature and Criticism*. London: Routledge, 1990.

Craige, Betty Jean. *Reconnection: Dualism to Holism in Literary Study*. Athens: The University of Georgia Press, 1988.

Durant, Alan and Nigel Fabb. *Literary Studies in Action*. London: Routledge, 1990.

Eagleton, Terry. *Literary Theory*. Oxford: Basil Blackwell, 1983.

Edwards, Paul, ed. *The Encyclopedia of Philosophy*. 1967. New York: Macmillan Publishing Co. & The Free Press, 1972.

Eliot, T.S. *To Criticise the Critic and Other Writings*. London: Faber and Faber Ltd., 1965.

______. *Notes Towards a Definition of Culture*. London: Faber and Faber Ltd., 1948.

______. *On Poetry and Poets*. London: Faber and Faber Ltd., 1957.

______. *Selected Essays*. 1934. London: Faber and Faber, 1966.

______. *The Use of Poetry and the Use of Criticism*. London: Faber and Faber, 1965.

Evans, Colin. *English People: The Experience of Teaching and Learning English in British Universities*. Buckingham: Open University Press, 1933.

Foucault, Michel. *The Foucault Reader*. Ed. Paul Rabinow. Harmondsworth: Penguin Books, 1984.

French, Philip. *Three Honest Men: A Critical Mosaic*. Manchester: Carcanet New Press, 1980.

Goodson, A.C. *Verbal Imagination: Coleridge & the Language of Modern Criticism*. New York: Oxford University Press, 1988.

Graver, S. *George Eliot and Community*. Berkeley: University of California Press, 1984.

Grene, Marjorie. *The Knower and the Known*. 1966. Berkeley: University of California Press, 1974.

Gross, John. *The Rise and Fall of the Man of Letters: English Literary Life since 1800*. Harmondsworth: Penguin, 1969.

Gunton, Sharon R., ed. *Contemporary Literary Criticism*. Michigan: Gale Research Company, 1983.

Hall, John. *The Sociology of Literature*. London: Longman, 1979.

Harris, Wendell V. *Dictionary of Concepts in Literary Criticism and Theory*. New York: Greenwood Press, 1992.

Hartman, Geoffrey H. *Criticism in the Wilderness: The Study of Literature*. New Haven: Yale University Press, 1980.

Hayman, Ronald. *Leavis*. London: Heinemann, 1976.

Johnson, Lesley. *The Cultural Critics: From Matthew Arnold to Raymond Williams*. London: Routledge & Kegan Paul, 1979.

Kojecky, Roger. *T.S. Eliot's Social Criticism*. New York: Farrar, Strauss and Giroux, 1971.

Kolakowski, Leszek. *Positivist Philosophy: From Hume to the Vienna Circle*. Trans. Norbert Guterman. 1968. Harmondsworth: Penguin Books, 1972.

Leavis, F.R. *Anna Karenina and Other Essays*. 1967. London: Chatto & Windus, 1973.

______. *The Common Pursuit*. 1952. London: Chatto & Windus, 1958.

______. *D.H. Lawrence: Novelist*. 1955. Harmondsworth: Penguin Books. 1981.

______. *Education and the University: A Sketch for an* 'English School.' London: Chatto & Windus, 1943.

______. *English Literature in Our Time and the University: Clark Lectures, 1967*. London: Chatto & Windus, 1969.

______. *The Great Tradition*. 1948. Harmondsworth: Penguin Books. 1980.

______. *The Critic as Anti-Philosopher*. Ed. G.S. Singh. London: Chatto & Windus, 1982.

______. *Letters in Criticism*. Ed. John Tasker. London: Chatto & Windus, 1974.

______. *The Living Principle: English as a Discipline of Thought*. London: Chatto & Windus, 1977.

______. *New Bearings in English Poetry: A Study of the Contemporary Situation*. 1932. London: Chatto & Windus, 1961.

______. *Nor Shall My Sword: Discourses on Pluralism, Compassion and Social Hope*. London: Chatto & Windus, 1972.

______. *Reading Out Poetry and Eugenio Montale—A Tribute*. Belfast: Mayne, Boyd & Son Ltd., 1979.

______. *Revaluation: Tradition and Development in English Poetry*. 1936. London: Chatto & Windus, 1969.

______. A Selection from *Scrutiny*. Cambridge: Cambridge University Press, 1968.

______. *Thought, Words and Creativity: Art and Thought in Lawrence*. New York: Oxford University Press, 1976.

______, ed. *Towards Standards of Criticism: Selections from the Calendar of Modern Letters (1925-27)*. 1933. London: Johnson Reprint Co., 1969..

______. *Valuation in Criticism and Other Essays*. Ed. G.S. Singh. Cambridge: Cambridge University Press. 1986.

Leavis, F.R. and Denys Thompson. *Culture and Environment: The Training of Critical Awareness*. London: Chatto and Windus, 1933.

Leavis, F.R. and Q.D. Leavis. *Dickens, the Novelist*. 1970. Harmondsworth: Penguin Books. 1980.

______. *Lectures in America*. London: Chatto & Windus, 1969.

Leavis, Q.D. *Fiction and the Reading Public*. 1932. London: Chatto & Windus, 1965.

Lucas, John. *Moderns & Contemporaries: Novelists, Poets and Critics*. Sussex: The Harvester Press, 1985.

MacCabe, Colin. *Theoretical Essays: Film, Linguistics and Literature*. Manchester: Manchester University Press, 1985.

McCallum, Pamela. *Literature and Method: Towards a Critique of I.A. Richards, T.S. Eliot and F.R. Leavis*. Dublin: Gill and Macmillan, 1983.

McMurtry, Jo. *English Language, English Literature: The Creation of an Academic Discipline*. London: Mansel Publishing Limited, 1985.

Mannheim, Karl. *Essays on Sociology and Social Psychology*. Ed. Paul Kecskemeti. London: Routledge & Kegan Paul Ltd., 1953.

Markova, Ivana. *Paradigms, Thought, and Language*. Chichuter: John Wiley & Sons, 1982.

Mathieson, Margaret. *The Preachers of Culture: A Study of English and its Teachers*. London: George Allen & Unwin Ltd., 1975.

Michael, Ian. *The Teaching of English: From the Sixteenth Century to 1870*. Cambridge: Cambridge University Press, 1987.

Mulhern, Francis. *The Moment of 'Scrutiny.'* London: N.L.B., 1979.

Narasimhaiah, C.D., ed. *F.R. Leavis: Some Aspects of His Work*. Mysore: Rao & Raghavan, 1963.

Needham, John. *The Completest Mode: I.A. Richards and Continuity of English Literary Criticism*. Edinburgh: University Press, 1982.

*The Open University: Arts: A Third Level Course*. Milton Keynes: Open University Press, 1976.

Panichas, George A. *The Reverent Discipline: Essays in Literary Criticism and Culture*. Knoxville: University of Tennessee Press, 1974.

Parkinson, G.H.R., ed. *An Encyclopaedia of Philosophy*. London: Routledge, 1988.

Polanyi, Michael. *Knowing and Being: Essays by Michael Polanyi*. Ed. Marjorie Grene. London: Routledge & Kegan Paul, 1969.

Priestley, J.B. *Thoughts in the Wilderness*. London: Heinemann, 1957.

Pritchard, William H. *Seeing through Everything: English Writers 1918-40*. London: Faber & Faber, 1977.

Quinton, Anthony. *Thoughts and Thinkers*. London: Duckworth, 1982.

Radford, Colin, and Sally Minogue. *The Nature of Criticism*. Sussex: The Harvester Press, 1981.

Rahv, Philip. *Literature and the Sixth Sense*. Boston: Houghton Mifflin Co., 1969.

Redfield, Robert. *The Little Community and Peasant Society and Culture*. Chicago: The University of Chicago Press, 1956.

Richards, I.A. *How to Read a Page*. 1943. London: Routledge & Kegan Paul,1967.

______. *Practical Criticism: A Study of Literary Judgment*. London: Routledge & Kegan Paul Ltd., 1929.

______. *Principles of Literary Criticism*. 1924. London: Routledge & Kegan Paul, 1970.

Robertson, P.J.M. *The Leavises on Fiction*. London: Chatto & Windus, 1981.

Robson, W.W. *Critical Essays*. London: Routledge & Kegan Paul, 1966.

______. *Modern English Literature*. London: Oxford University Press, 1978.

Samson, Anne. *F.R. Leavis*. New York: Harvester Wheatsheaf, 1992.

Sills, David L., ed. *International Encyclopedia of Social Sciences*. New York: Macmillan & The Free Press, 1972.

Singh, G.S., ed. *The Critic as Anti-Philosopher*. London: Chatto & Windus, 1982.

______. *English Miscellany: A Symposium of History, Literature and the Arts*. Ed. Mario Praz. Rome: Edizioni Di Storia E Letteratura, 1965.

______, ed. *Valuation in Criticism and Other Essays*. Cambridge: Cam-

bridge University Press, 1986.
Sridhar, M. *The Concept of Organic Community as a Criterion in F.R. Leavis's Criticism*. M. Litt. Diss. CIEFL, 1988.
Steiner, George. *Language and Silence*. Harmondsworth: Penguin, 1967.
Sturt, George. *The Wheelwright's Shop*. 1923. Cambridge: Cambridge University Press, 1980.
Swingewood, Alan. *The Myth of Mass Culture*. London: Macmillan, 1977.
Symons, Julien. *Critical Observations*. London: Faber & Faber, 1981.
*The Teaching of English in England*. London: His Majesty's Stationery Office (HMSO), 1926.
Theodorson, George and Achilles Theodorson, eds. *A Modern Dictionary of Sociology*. New York: Barnes & Noble Books, 1979.
Thompson, Denys, ed. *The Leavises: Recollections and Impressions*. Cambridge: Cambridge University Press, 1984.
Thompson, E.P. *The Making of the English Working Class*. New York: Vintage Books, 1966.
Thornton, R.K.R. *The Decadent Dilemma*. London: Edward Arnold, 1983.
*The Times Literary Supplement, 1967*. Vol. 6. London: Oxford University Press, 1968.
Tillyard, E.M.W. *The Muse Unchained: An Intimate Account of the Revolution in English Studies in Cambridge*. London: Bowes & Bowes.
Trilling, Lionel. *Beyond Culture: Essays on Literature and Learning*. Harmondsworth: Penguin Books, 1965.
Turner, Victor. *From Ritual to Theatre: The Human Seriousness of Play*. New York: Performing Arts Journal Publications, 1982.
Volosinov, V.N. *Marxism and the Philosophy of Language*. Trans. Ladislav Matejka and I.R. Titunik. New York: Seminar Press, 1973.
Walsh, William. *A Human Idiom: Literature and Humanity*. London: Chatto & Windus, 1964.
______. *F.R. Leavis*. London: Chatto & Windus, 1980.
______. *The Use of Imagination: Educational Thought and the Literary Mind*. London: Chatto & Windus, 1964.
Watson, Garry. *The Leavises, The Social & The Left*. Swansea: Brynmill, 1977.
Watson, George. *The Literary Critics*. 1962. London: Chatto & Windus, 1964.
Widdowson, Peter. *Re-Reading English*. London: Methuen, 1982.
Williams, Raymond. *Culture and Society: 1780-1950*. 1961. Harmondsworth: Penguin Books, 1982.
______. *Key Words: A Vocabulary of Culture and Society*. 1976. London: Fontana Paperbacks, 1983.
Wilson, Sandy. *The Roaring Twenties*. London: Eyre Methuen, 1976.
Wordsworth, William and S.T. Coleridge. *Lyrical Ballads 1798*. Ed. W.J.B. Owen. 1969. London: Oxford University Press. 1976.